Exploring Languages

A Complete Introduction for Foreign Language Students

Dora F. Kennedy
University of Maryland, College Park, MD
Prince George's County, MD, Public Schools (retired)

Pat Barr-Harrison
Prince George's County, MD, Public Schools

Leslie M. Grahn
Benjamin Tasker Middle School, Bowie, MD

National Textbook Company
a division of *NTC Publishing Group* • Lincolnwood, Illinois USA

Contents

Foreword   v

INTRODUCTION   **1**

Goals and Models of Foreign Language Exploratory Courses   3
General Description of *Exploring Languages*   4
Planning an Exploratory Program   5

METHODOLOGY   **7**

Using This Teacher's Manual   9
Implementing *Exploring Languages* in the Classroom   9
Language Learning Strategies and Activities   11
General List of Classroom/Homework Activities   14
Assessment   14
Cooperative Learning in the Exploratory Classroom   16
Exploring Languages and General Curricular Trends   18
General Teacher Reference Materials   23

TEACHING THE CHAPTERS   **25**

Chapter 1   Communicating for World Understanding   27
Chapter 2   Signs and Symbols, including Esperanto   31
Chapter 3   Your Language and Mine and How It Came to Be   36
Chapter 4   Families of Languages: Their Similarities and Differences   41
Chapter 5   Exploring Spanish and the Hispanic World   44
Chapter 6   Exploring French and the French-Speaking World   49
Chapter 7   Exploring German and German-Speaking Areas   56
Chapter 8   Exploring Italian, Italy, and Its People   61
Chapter 9   Exploring Russian, Russia, and Its People   66
Chapter 10   Exploring Japanese, Japan, and Its People   71
Chapter 11   Exploring Chinese, China, and Its People   78
Chapter 12   Exploring Arabic and the Arabic-Speaking World   83
Chapter 13   Exploring the Hebrew Language, Israel, and Its People   88
Chapter 14   Exploring Swahili and Swahili-Speaking Areas   92
Chapter 15   Exploring Latin, Ancient Rome, and Its People   100
Chapter 16   Exploring Ancient Greek and the Ancient Greek World   106

Appendix A   **Master Address List**   **115**
Appendix B   **Course Pretest and Posttest**   **119**
Appendix C   **Student Activity Pages - Answer Key**   **123**
Appendix D   **Student Activity Pages**   **133**

The Ambiance of the Foreign Language Exploratory Class

Teachers of foreign language exploratory courses should foster an atmosphere of inquisitiveness about words and their meanings, about languages and cultures, about the phenomenon of language. They should use amusing as well as intellectually challenging activities, such as "word detectives," "mystery words," and puzzles. They should nourish the notion that they and their students are a team in the pursuit of the world view.

Acquiring a broad base of language functioning is good preparation for in-depth and more formal study of a foreign language.

Foreword

Foreign language exploratory courses have existed in one form or another from the 1910s to the present. The focus and objectives of these courses have undergone a metamorphosis over the years, reflecting changes in societal and developmental needs of emerging adolescents—the primary audience for these programs.

In earlier years of their existence, exploratory courses were almost exclusively designed to offer late elementary and junior high school students a "smattering" of several foreign languages for the sole purpose of helping them decide which languages to study in high school.

While a few schools may still cling to the above rationale, many are stepping into the twenty-first century and are offering a *new, more diverse* exploratory curriculum—one that continues to be not only self-contained and nonsequential, but also *interdisciplinary* in nature. The new exploratory curriculum can include the exploration of both commonly and uncommonly taught languages and cultures, as well as invented languages. It complements the "global education" concept and is in keeping with the current middle school philosophy of exploration. It encourages foreign language study and initiates students into this discipline.

This manual is designed to enhance the teacher's use of the text *Exploring Languages*, which is intended for the middle and junior high school levels. This practical teacher's guide to the structure and utilization of the text presents overall methodology, exploratory goals, objectives, and outcomes envisioned for each chapter, plus activities to supplement the text. It includes information beyond the text and a list of resources and references. A key is provided for the questions and activities in each chapter. A student activity sheet is provided for most chapters, suitable for reproduction.

William E. De Lorenzo
College of Education
University of Maryland
College Park, Maryland

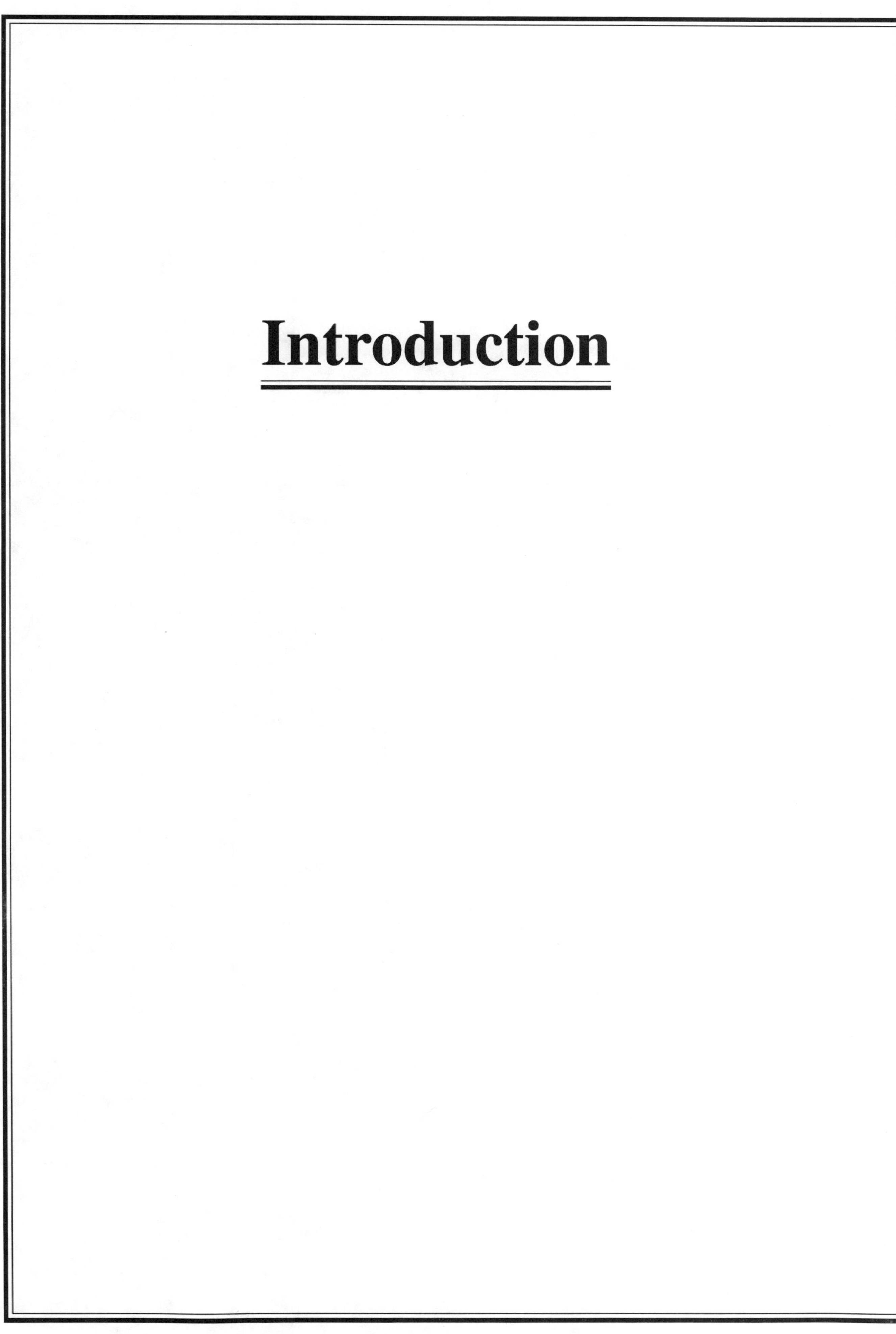

Introduction

GOALS AND MODELS OF FOREIGN LANGUAGE EXPLORATORY COURSES

Exploring Languages is a text to be used in foreign language exploratory programs, mainly in middle schools. Among the most important goals of such programs, commonly known as FLEX programs, are these:

1. Building readiness for the study of languages and cultures in a classroom setting
2. Introducing students to the concept of relationships among languages (language connections)
3. Helping students develop language learning strategies (related to metacognition in the teaching of thinking skills)
4. Developing positive attitudes toward other cultures
5. Developing appreciation of one's own heritage and the American goal of unity in diversity
6. Reinforcing English literacy skills and vocabulary
7. Widening students' horizons with regard to languages and the world of work in a global perspective

It is in the framework of these overall goals that the objectives and outcomes of specific chapters in *Exploring Languages* function. These goals are to be kept in mind when working with any exploratory program.

Exploratory programs usually follow one of the following models:

- *A general language model* acts as an introduction to the phenomenon of language, its development, language families, and language relationships.

- *A language sampler model* provides experiences with one or more languages and cultures, with limited, "preproficiency" objectives with regard to language skills.

- *An integrated model* includes both of the above components. This is the most common.

Regardless of model, minimum outcomes should be clearly defined as to speaking, reading, recognition of languages, and level of writing, including copying. Well-planned exploratory courses can be invaluable in providing many middle school or upper elementary students with a background for foreign language study in a classroom setting. They are especially, but not exclusively, helpful to at-risk students and those in need of academic enrichment.

Exploratory programs should be interdisciplinary, emphasizing the interconnectedness of the curriculum, and should raise students' level of awareness about language and improve their skills and knowledge of English as part of linguistic development. As a subsidiary goal, they help students develop career awareness. (For a thorough discussion of exploratory courses, see *Complete Guide to Exploratory Language Programs*, Dora F. Kennedy and William De Lorenzo, National Textbook, 1985).

GENERAL DESCRIPTION OF
EXPLORING LANGUAGES

Exploring Languages can be used in all of the following types of programs or program models:

1. A general introduction to language (general language model)
2. A foreign language sampler model ("language potpourri")
3. An integrated program, combining a general introduction to language, together with presentation of specific languages
4. Programs that introduce only one language
5. A social studies or language arts program with a *global education perspective*

Organization of the Text

Exploring Languages includes sixteen chapters. There are two main sections: *Part 1, Exploring the World of Language,* which introduces general concepts about language, and *Part 2, Exploring the Languages of the World*, which provides information and experiences about a variety of languages. The text can be used sequentially or nonsequentially, depending on the nature of the individual school's program.

Here is an overview of the contents of the two parts.

Part 1, Exploring the World of Language

*   The first chapter serves as a general introduction to the concept of languages and communication. (It should be taught first no matter what the program model.)
*   Chapters 2 to 4 cover general language concepts, signs and symbols in communication, invented languages (including Esperanto), the history of English, origins of American place names, and language families.

Part 2, Exploring the Languages of the World

*   Chapters 5 to 16 each explore a specific language: Spanish, French, German, Italian, Russian, Japanese, Chinese, Arabic, Hebrew, Swahili, Latin, ancient Greek. These chapters contain background information about the language and the culture in which it is (or was) spoken, as well as some basic words and phrases in the language.

In summary, part 1 contains what can be called the general language component of an exploratory program, while part 2 contains the language sampler component. The information in part 2 also serves to reinforce general language concepts as they are illustrated through a specific language; for example, the language's connections with English can be emphasized, thus reinforcing English vocabulary.

PLANNING AN EXPLORATORY PROGRAM

Deciding on a program model is essential to any FLEX program, whether general language, foreign language sampler, or integrated. Here are some general guidelines to consider in setting up a FLEX program.

Recommendations for Administrators

1. Consider the exploratory course as a part of the foreign language curriculum.

2. Assign only foreign language majors to teach exploratory courses. (Experience in many school districts has shown that foreign language majors tend to acquire survival skills in other languages more easily than those who have never studied a foreign language [Kennedy and De Lorenzo, p. 86]. In addition, it is desirable for schools to employ foreign language majors who have studied additional languages, albeit informally.)

3. Explain the nature of the program to students, parents, other administrators, counselors, and school staff.

4. Regardless of the length or type of exploratory course, *daily* instruction is most productive.

5. Encourage interdisciplinary efforts between the FLEX teachers and other teachers, particularly teachers of art, music, language arts, and social studies.

Recommendations for Teachers

1. Establish a program model, curriculum framework, and timetable with specific goals, objectives, and outcomes. This includes planning which languages are to be explored and for how long a time. (To perform this task, refer to the *Exploring Languages* text, as well as this teacher's manual. A good starting point is the Methodology section of this manual.)

2. Decide on standards for the course. These are to be discussed with students. The exploratory class is to be considered an academic subject and should not be viewed as "frivolous fun and games." It is rightly considered as different from formal language courses, but should not be considered as academically less worthy.

3. Use a *student-centered, hands-on approach* in the classroom as much as possible. This manual contains many helpful suggestions to promote student involvement.

4. Emerging school system priorities such as multicultural education and critical thinking can and should be developed in the exploratory program. (See the section *Exploring Languages* and General Curricular Trends, pages 18 to 23 in this manual, for more information on integrating these goals into the FLEX program.)

5. Avoid teaching the sampler during the entire class period, as in a level I language class. This defeats the broad educational goals of the exploratory concept.

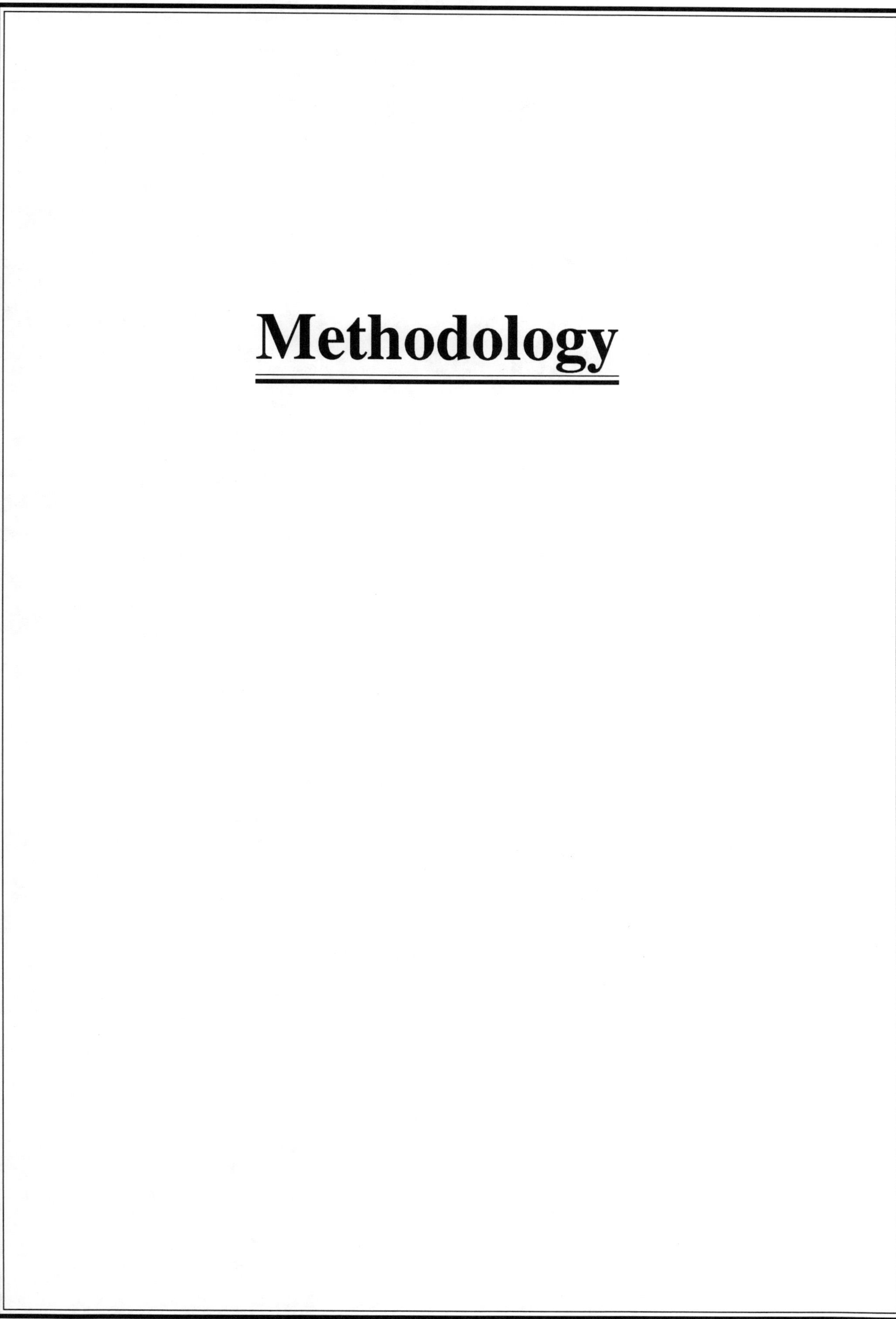

Methodology

USING THIS TEACHER'S MANUAL

This teacher's manual is an essential tool and resource in implementing *Exploring Languages* in the classroom. It provides a wealth of strategies and activities for use in the classroom.

Outline of the Manual

Here is a general outline of contents of the teacher's manual:

- **Introduction**

  It describes goals and models of FLEX programs and gives an overview of the *Exploring Languages* text.

- **Methodology**

  This presents a plan for daily classroom instruction. It includes practical suggestions for teaching specific language skills in the foreign languages: vocabulary, structural awareness, listening, speaking, reading, writing. It describes assessment procedures. It also suggests ways to promote cooperative learning in the classroom.

- ***Exploring Languages* and General Curricular Goals**

  Suggestions are provided for using *Exploring Languages* to teach to the following curricular goals: multicultural education, global awareness, career awareness, critical thinking.

- **Teaching the Chapters**

  Detailed suggestions are given for teaching each chapter in the text, including its goal and outcomes/objectives, suggestions for presenting the chapter, follow-up activities, an answer key, supplementary information, and resources and materials to supplement the text.

IMPLEMENTING *EXPLORING LANGUAGES* IN THE CLASSROOM

Exploring Languages need not be taught in a particular sequence. The chapters to be covered in class will depend on the program model and languages selected. It is recommended, however, that chapter 1, Communicating for World Understanding, be taught at the beginning of the course regardless of the exploratory program model in order to establish a framework for the study of world languages.

Recommended Procedures

Beginning-of-Course Strategies

1. "Walk" students through the *Exploring Languages* text. Have students take an "inventory" of the text to become acquainted with it. Have them look for the table of contents, chapter titles, index. Ask students to find certain information.

   Examples: In what chapter would you study about Spanish? English? In what chapter would you find a language family tree? How do you know?

2. Administer a pretest on cultural and linguistic concepts. See Appendix B. Explain to students that they will learn answers to the questions as they work in the exploratory course. Have students take the posttest after completing the course and compare their answers.

3. From the first day of instruction, introduce some expressions, such as greetings, from languages to be explored. This procedure serves to establish a higher level of interest. (Students come to the course expecting to learn to "say something" from the beginning.)

4. Have the class establish a pen pal relationship with another FLEX class in the school, the school system, or elsewhere. Students write letters and compositions telling their pen pals what they are doing in class, what languages they are exploring, and so on. Plan exchanges with the pen pals, such an end-of-year get-together, if feasible.

Strategies for Working with Language Chapters

Below is a lesson plan model for use in presenting chapters 5 to 16, which focus on individual languages. This plan is set up for a 50-minute period and assumes an integrated type of FLEX course.

1. Practicing the Language (15 minutes)
   Activities may include warm-up, review, speaking, reading recognition, listening, role-playing, and copying words in the foreign language. The teacher conducts this in the language if possible. (See Language Learning Activities and Strategies, on pages 11 to 13, for a wide range of activities for language practice.)

2. Discussing the Language (5 minutes)
   Activities include studying language connections (English words borrowed or derived from the language or vice versa) and discussion of language learning strategies.

3. Exploring Culture (25 minutes)
   Activities include reports, projects, discussions, reading in the text, reading supplementary texts, writing letters for information. It is in this part of the lesson in which career awareness and multicultural education can be infused.

4. Closure Activities (5 minutes)
   Activities include planning together (teacher/class), assignment/questions, evaluation of work period, quick review of language elements studied, singing. Homework should be assigned in FLEX classes. (See the General List of Class/Homework Activities, page 14, for examples of homework assignments.)

Important Notes on Working with Language Chapters

1. The language chapters are intended only as an *introduction* to the language, as an exposure before a Level I course. They help develop readiness for language study. This approach may be especially helpful for the student who plans to study one of the less commonly taught languages, such as Russian and Japanese.

2. Pronunciation aids are given in all of the language chapters to enable students to work independently in the text. The transcriptions are, of course, approximations aimed at helping English-speaking learners say words in foreign languages. They are not intended to be linguistically

precise, scientific pronunciations. The pronunciation aids are included for the commonly taught languages such as Spanish, French, and German, since not all teachers may be conversant in all the languages.

3. Although the objectives and outcomes for each chapter are given in this manual, these are suggestive: "a floor, not a ceiling." The teacher who is fluent in a particular language is encouraged to go beyond the material in the chapter. The teacher would conduct the "Practicing the Language" segment of the class in the foreign language. Students in such an exploratory class might attain novice-low on the ACTFL proficiency guidelines. *However, it should be emphasized that an exploratory course is not a traditional language course.* The other objectives of an exploratory course, such as cultural topics, nature of language, English and foreign word connections, should not be ignored.

4. Use the exploratory program as a context in which students can improve their reading, writing, and research skills in English. In the exploratory course, in the Exploring Culture segment, students are provided with opportunities to use English. Make sure that students understand that high standards are to be maintained in all the work they do in their exploratory class.

5. Refer to Language Learning Strategies and Activities, pages 11 to 13, for many concrete suggestions for implementing the foreign language portion of *Exploring Languages.*

LANGUAGE LEARNING STRATEGIES AND ACTIVITIES

One of the outcomes of an exploratory language program should be an increased readiness on the part of students to study foreign languages. However, this outcome depends on the degree to which the teacher emphasizes language learning strategies and engages students in activities that incorporate these strategies.

This section contains a list of strategies and activities that can make the exploratory course the "prep" class for later foreign language study. In teaching each chapter in *Exploring Languages*, you may choose from among the strategies and activities or have students choose on their own. You may want to add your own, as they suit your personal style and the learning styles of your students.

Activities for Learning Vocabulary

The activities below are ones that students can do to learn vocabulary in a foreign language.

1. Make picture dictionaries with words from the foreign language

2. Make word-family posters (with teacher guidance)

   Examples:

   a. French: *Bon*, with English connections, *bonbons* (candy); *bon voyage*; *Bon Ami* (product); *bon appétit*; and so on. Have students keep in mind that *bon* means "good."

   b. Latin: *Amare* (Love) poster, with English connections (*amiable, amity*); other language connections (*amigo/a*, Spanish; *ami*, French; *amico/a*, Italian). Have students illustrate the poster.

3. Develop vocabulary "cheers" or "raps" and recite them together in class. Some raps could incorporate foreign language words and their definitions in English.

4. Work vocabulary words into familiar tunes, such as "Row, Row, Row Your Boat"

5. Do charades, in which students guess the words being acted out, using the foreign language

6. Write and present skits or "stories" built around vocabulary words

7. Label objects in the classroom with the words in the foreign language

8. Play standard vocabulary games: hangman, vocabulary bee, crossword, word search

Strategies for Grammatical Awareness

It is recommended that teachers indicate some basic points about the structure of language as students are introduced to words and phrases in specific languages. Some specific grammatical points are:

- word order (position of nouns and verbs, nouns and adjectives)
- use of pronouns
- singular vs. plural
- gender of nouns

These points are developed through the "teachable moment," for example, by mentioning that *amiga* in Spanish is used for a girl or woman, *amigo* for a man; that *la* in Spanish is used for nouns that are feminine in gender, *el* for nouns that are masculine.

Another way to help students develop an appreciation for the structure of language is to have them "invent" a language, a favorite FLEX activity in the middle school.

Caveat: The sophistication of the explanations should reflect the age and level of awareness of students. Explanations should not be complex.

Strategies for Teaching Listening Skills

The listening component should help students become aware of the differences in sounds and rhythm among languages.

The teacher may devise exercises or games in which students do activities like these:

1. Identify the words or expressions heard

2. Listen to a small amount of authentic language to experience the flow of the language

3. Respond to commands given in the language. See, for example, the Spanish chapter. This method of language learning, by responding to commands, is known as Total Physical Response (TPR) and was developed by James Asher.

4. Identify which language is being spoken (after several languages have been explored)

Strategies for Teaching Speaking Skills

In general, the major focus of the FLEX language lesson is the speaking segment. Although speaking is limited to designated material in the novice-low range of proficiency, the teacher is encouraged to devise activities that help students retain the material as communicative rather than as isolated bits. For example, numbers can be incorporated into math problems, or students can read out telephone numbers or addresses. The aim should be repetition in a variety of contexts to order to facilitate students' retention and fluency.

The teacher may devise hands-on activities like those below:

1. *Role-plays.* Students use any dialogues in the text, and the teacher and students may create additional dialogues that incorporate studied words.

2. *Simulations.* These could include restaurant and classroom scenes.

3. *Teaching experiences.* Students teach important words or phrases to other classes or to family members.

Strategies for Teaching Reading and Writing

The main reading goal of an exploratory course is recognition of a designated body of material in a foreign language, with comprehension of those items that are taught intensively. To do this, the teacher uses the material in the text. As far as writing, the main activity is copying words and expressions. Copying helps students develop recognition for reading and can be regarded as a skill that builds readiness for foreign language study. Simple guided sentence writing may be incorporated, particularly in the case of commonly taught languages such as Spanish and French.

To implement general reading and writing goals, here are some suggested activities for students to do:

1. Scan authentic materials such as ethnic restaurant menus, transportation schedules, television program charts, travel postcards and travel literature, and foreign newspapers, for words that they know or recognize

2. Create menus and postcards, using words from the foreign language

3. Look at ads from newspapers and magazines in the target language to identify words they know and to guess what the ad is selling

4. Work with simple dialogues from foreign language texts

5. Work to write simple sentences in the foreign language, using all that they have learned both in the text and beyond the text

6. Given printed paragraphs of languages studied, determine the language in which the paragraph is written

7. For languages with non-Roman alphabets (Russian, Arabic, Hebrew, Greek), make large replicas of the letters on posters or out of papier-mâché or cardboard and paint them. (As students manipulate the symbols, they learn to recognize and write them. Students can do similar activities for characters in nonalphabetic languages, such as Chinese and Japanese.)

GENERAL LIST OF CLASSROOM/HOMEWORK ACTIVITIES

Here is a list of general activities and language learning activities that can be used for various chapters in the text. Many of these can be done as homework. Others are more suitable for in-class work. The suggestions for teaching each chapter contain more such activities. Be sure to establish standards for all work to be handed in.

1. Answer questions and complete projects suggested in the text
2. Keep a personal notebook for special notes, vocabulary, new English words, language connections, and special assignments (Students may develop their notebook with teacher guidance.)
3. Listen to the evening news and make lists of all foreign names and places mentioned
4. Listen to commercials for foreign words and expressions
5. Draw maps and fill in outline maps
6. Interview someone in the community who is a native speaker of the language being explored
7. Create vocabulary games to do in class, for example, crossword puzzles or word search puzzles incorporating the foreign words
8. Create charts, games, etc., to help in teaching the class and learning words and expressions
9. Make travel brochures and menus
10. Prepare a research booklet on a country to include: interesting facts, maps, drawings, photos, basic expressions in the language, recipes, songs
11. Do cooking or food projects and collect recipes
12. Create skits or role-plays in the foreign language. These may be video-taped. Puppets may be used.
13. Make dioramas, showing places in the foreign country
14. Write a group composition or story. The story might be about a trip to a country or a historic event.
15. Play "Who Am I?" game. Student describes a famous person from the country or culture explored. The class guesses who it is. (Students may even wear clothes or costumes appropriate for the famous person.) In a variation of the activity, names of famous persons are pinned to the backs of students. Students interview one another to find out who they are.
16. Use student-made materials as teaching devices.

ASSESSMENT

Tests in an exploratory course should reflect the specific objectives and material taught. For example, students should not be asked to produce vocabulary items that were taught for recognition only.

In an integrated exploratory course, these are general items to be tested:

- words and phrases in the language explored
- cultural details taught for retention

- general facts about the language being explored
- readiness for foreign language learning
- concepts of language and culture
- English derivatives and borrowed words, cognates

Here are specific language skills to be tested:

1. Listening comprehension

   Test only the specific items taught. Test for general recognition of differences between languages.

2. Speaking

   Test words and phrases taught, in a situational context.

3. Reading

   Test for recognition of words/phrases taught and for minimal comprehension of simple connected discourse.

4. Writing

   a. Copying correctly

   b. Spelling from memory: persons and places, designated words from the foreign language, related words in English

General Testing

Here are some suggestions for designing various types of classroom tests for *Exploring Languages*.

1. Use the list of objectives/outcomes for each chapter, given in this manual, as the basis for testing.

2. Use most of the conventional types of teacher-made tests and quizzes, such as recall, true-false, completion, multiple-choice, short answer, and essay. Tests may be oral, one-on-one tests that simulate conversational exchanges.

3. Give frequent short quizzes. No test should take an entire class period.

4. Go over a test as soon as possible after students have completed it. Tests should provide a learning experience.

5. Seek innovative ways of testing. For example, in a multiple-choice test, students may be asked to write statements defending their answers.

Assessing Performance

The exploratory course lends itself to the performance assessment approach to testing. The byword is not only "What do students *know*?" but "What are students able to *do*?" Hence, in addition to paper-and-pencil and oral testing, the teacher may assign special projects or set up contexts in which students are to apply what they have learned. See the French Greetings Quiz in Figure 1 on page 16.

One of the most useful approaches to performance assessment is the development of a portfolio by every student. The portfolio includes samples of the student's performance, which document the students' use of skills and knowledge acquired.

Figure 1

Sample French Greetings Quiz

This is a sample quiz that can be given in the conventional manner by having students write the answers or in the "performance assessment" mode by having students give oral answers in a social context.

1. You meet a friend. What can you say?
2. When you leave a room, what can you say?
3. A friend asks you how you are. What can you say?
4. When you want to introduce a friend to someone, what do you say?
5. When you want to introduce yourself, what can you say?
6. When you want to find out someone's name, what can you say?
7. When you want to tell someone where you live, what can you say?
8. You want to ask a friend how he or she is. What can you say?

Related References

"Connecting Testing and Learning in the Classroom and on the Program Level," by Elana Shohamy, *Northeast Conference Reports*, 1991.

Using Performance Assessment, *Educational Leadership*, May 1992. (Entire issue)

COOPERATIVE LEARNING IN THE EXPLORATORY CLASSROOM

Cooperative learning occurs when students work in groups to perform a task together, sharing information. A main objective of cooperative learning is to promote maximum productivity for the time spent in the classroom. Students are actively involved as they work in groups. At the same time, students are learning group/social skills.

Many forms of grouping, structures, or teams have been devised for cooperative learning. (See the Related References at the end of this discussion.) The exploratory class lends itself to cooperative learning; for example, for projects and for language learning activities. However, cooperative learning formats should not be used exclusively. "There should be a happy balance of cooperative, competitive, and individualistic classroom structures in order to prepare students for the full range of social situations" (Spencer Kagan).

Some "social" benefits of cooperative learning can be students who:

1. Are supportive of one another in class

2. Follow through on group and individual tasks

3. Have better developed social, interactive skills in addition to the command of the material being learned

4. Have enhanced self-esteem

Establishing Cooperative Learning Groups

Here are some general recommendations for setting up cooperative learning groups:

1. Each group should be heterogeneous, made up of four to five students, representing a range of abilities, from highest to lowest achieving.

2. The rationale for cooperative learning is that students help one another. Slower students can achieve success by working with high achievers. High achievers are challenged to share their knowledge and learning strategies. *There should also be challenges to additional learning for high achievers.*

3. Despite the group setting, students should understand that grading is based on individual achievement and effort. Students should be held responsible for their own learning, plus their contribution to the group effort. There may be rewards at times in order to enhance motivation.

4. Since working in cooperative groups requires social interaction, students should practice different group activities before going into cooperative learning groups per se.

5. Teachers and students together should establish standards for working in the cooperative learning setting.

6. Groups should be reorganized periodically, e.g., every six to eight weeks or grading period.

7. The teacher must adapt material so that it is suited to the group format.

Examples of Cooperative Learning Structures

1. Roundrobin

   Each student is required to share some information with a teammate to do a task, e.g., list famous people from a culture, list famous places in a country, list the numbers from 1-10 in the foreign language.

2. Numbered Heads Together

   The teacher asks a question or provides an activity; students (in groups) consult to make sure that everyone knows the answer; one student in the group is called on to answer. (This format is appropriate for review of lesson material and for listening or reading comprehension.)

3. Think-Pair-Share

   The teacher asks a question or provides a topic; students pair up to discuss it; pairs share their thoughts with the class.

4. Projects

   Here are suggested steps for cooperative projects:

   Stage One: Identify the tasks and organize students into groups with assigned tasks

   Stage Two: Group members plan their tasks

   Stage Three: Members carry out the tasks

   Stage Four: Members work together to prepare report

   Stage Five: Members present report

   Stage Six: Evaluation

Related References

Cooperative Learning: Resources for Teaching, by Spencer Kagan, Resources for Teachers, 1989.

"Cooperative Learning: Can Students Help Students Learn?," *Instructor Magazine*, March 1987, pp. 74-78.

Cooperative Learning. *Educational Leadership*, December 1989/January 1990. (Entire issue)

Using Student Team Learning, by Robert E. Slavin, Center for the Social Organization of Schools, The Johns Hopkins University, 1986.

EXPLORING LANGUAGES AND GENERAL CURRICULAR TRENDS

Multicultural Education

Exploring Languages is by its very nature multicultural. The term "multicultural education," as mandated by an increasing number of school systems, refers specifically to developing student awareness of cultural diversity in the United States and to fostering the American ideal of unity in diversity. Multicultural education involves helping students develop an understanding and appreciation of the contributions of many groups in the history of this country. An important outcome is that the diverse groups of students in a class "see" themselves reflected in the curriculum and instructional materials.

Exploring Languages is admirably suited to meeting the goal of multicultural education as described, as are most foreign language exploratory programs. The various languages and cultures reflected in the text help students develop awareness and appreciation of the diverse groups in our nation. For example, the Spanish chapter describes the importance of Hispanic culture in American society. The Swahili chapter discusses African culture, part of the background of African American society. The Chinese and Japanese chapters reflect the heritage of Asian Americans. The section of chapter 3 that focuses on place names describes some contributions of Native Americans. Most of the language chapters address the cultural heritage of Americans; for example, Americans who are of French heritage, Italian Americans, German Americans, Arab Americans, Jewish Americans, and so on.

Strategies

The chapters and/or the related activities in this manual focus not just on the country or culture of origin, but also on Americans who were born in that country or are part of that culture. Teachers should include the American-related material in their curriculum. For example, teachers should assign projects and reports that deal with African Americans, Asian Americans, and so on, in addition to those dealing with the countries and cultures themselves.

The text, thus, is an excellent vehicle for helping students develop a multicultural perspective and awareness of the dignity of each individual.

Related Reference

Educational Leadership, December 1991/January 1992. (Entire issue)

Global Education

The American folk philosopher, baseball player Yogi Berra, might have said, "The world is getting more and more global." An exploratory course is by its nature suited to helping students develop a global view. The precepts of global education, although usually implemented through the social studies curriculum, are also a part of FLEX courses. The precepts include:

1. Developing a global perspective, looking ahead to the twenty-first century
2. Developing an understanding and awareness of the interdependence of the peoples of the planet
3. Developing a concern for the welfare of the planet
4. Developing an awareness of the many cultures and languages of the world and their interconnectedness

Strategies

Central to the implementation of global education principles is the development of a positive attitude toward diverse cultures and toward the preservation of the planet. Global education is a perspective that is infused into the ongoing instructional program, rather than being a separate subject. Both teachers and students should develop a mind-set of a global view as they work on the activities suggested in the text. The teacher should consult with the social studies and science departments in order to achieve greater interdisciplinary cooperation in teaching of global concepts.

Related References

Global Education, (Yearbook), Association for Supervision and Curriculum Development, 1991.

"Global Education for the Twenty-first Century," by Siegfried Ramler, *Educational Leadership*, April 1991, pp. 44-49.

For general information on the topic of global education, write to the American Forum for Global Education, 45 John St., Suite 908, New York, NY 10038.

Development of Thinking Skills

The teaching of thinking skills has become a national priority. Many of the activities in *Exploring Languages* were generated with the purpose of helping students enhance their higher-level thinking skills, beyond the recall category.

There are three basic approaches advocated for the teaching of thinking skills and processes. Teachers must become convinced that thinking can be expressly taught.

1. Creating a classroom environment that fosters thinking without direct teaching of thinking skills
2. Infusing thinking skills into regular classroom instruction; in other words, teaching thinking skills in conjunction with subject matter
3. Separate courses for teaching thinking skills

FLEX teachers can incorporate the first two approaches in their classes. (See Strategies below for some specific suggestions.)

In working with the chapters in *Exploring Languages*, the teacher should keep in mind the following general information about the "dimensions of thinking."

1. Thinking is a process, rather than a fixed state.

   Examples for FLEX: Forming of concepts about the nature of language and different languages; making comparisons among languages explored; organizing information (writing reports); comprehending a new language

2. Thinking is creative and explores new situations.

   Example for FLEX: Opportunities to explore new cultures.

3. There are core thinking skills, which involve interpreting, analyzing, etc. Some are listed here.

   - Focusing: Attending to the selected or assigned task
   - Information gathering: By observing and researching
   - Remembering: Storing and retrieving information
   - Organizing: Arranging information (classifying, ordering, comparing, contrasting)
   - Analyzing: Identifying characteristics or parts, relationships, main ideas, errors
   - Generating: Producing new information, inferring, elaborating
   - Integrating: Summarizing, restructuring
   - Evaluating: Judging by criteria, verifying

   Examples for FLEX: The study of different languages lends itself to all of the thinking skills. Many of the activities in the text focus on the above processes. The teacher should encourage further use of them by class discussion, encouraging students to analyze, compare, summarize, and make inferences about what they are learning in the text.

4. Megacognition is the awareness of one's own thinking processes.

   Examples for FLEX: Discuss periodically with students how they arrived at a particular language connection or particular conclusion about language.

   In addition to using the "teachable moment" to incorporate thinking skills, the teacher should discuss them in conjunction with assignments and class tasks.

Strategies

Here are some specific strategies for incorporating thinking skills into an exploratory program:

1. Provide "wait time": at least five seconds of thinking after a question is asked.

2. Use questioning frequently: Why?, How do you know?, Give an example, and so on.

3. Ask questions that can have more than one answer. Ask students to justify their response.

4. Train students to *ask*, or generate, questions.

5. Use the think-pair-share strategy: Allow thinking time, sharing with a partner, followed by group discussion.

6. Ask students to discuss how they arrived at answers (metacognition).

7. Have students summarize a discussion (orally or in written form).

8. Have students use graphic organizers to compare or classify information.

Graphic Organizers

Graphic organizers are charts, circles, rectangles, or other visual representations used to help organize information and show relationships, including comparison and contrast.

Examples are Venn diagrams, sequence-of-events chains, main idea tables. Encourage students to produce their own graphic organizers once you and students have worked through several examples. See the samples in figures 2 and 3. Figure 2 shows a Venn diagram in which two cultures are compared and contrasted. Figure 3 shows a blank sequence-of-events chain. It could be used for topics such as the history of English or the history of one of the countries described in the chapters.

Related References

Dimensions of Thinking: A Framework for Curriculum and Instruction, by Robert J. Marzano et al., Association for Supervision and Curriculum Development, 1988.

Many materials on thinking skills are available from the Association for Supervision and Curriculum Development (see Appendix A, Master Address List).

Career Awareness

In the exploratory language class, students should be introduced to how foreign languages can be useful in the world of work. The curriculum in many middle schools and for the upper elementary grades calls for the exploration of various occupations. Students are encouraged to think about the relationship of their studies to future careers. To incorporate career awareness into the exploratory language classroom, the teacher can encourage students to do activities like the ones in the Strategies section below. The teacher might want to focus on languages that are most visible in the marketplace, e.g., Spanish, Japanese, German, French.

Strategies

1. Refer students to the chart on Foreign Languages and the World of Work in chapter 1 in the text. Have students expand the list of occupations and explain how knowing a foreign language can be useful in each job.

2. Point out how even a limited skill in a foreign language can be useful, e.g., for library work, newspaper reporting, communications.

3. Have students prepare their own foreign language and world of work chart. If the school has a career lab or resource center, have students refer to these.

4. Have students interview one person who uses a foreign language on the job, and have the person explain why knowing the foreign language is useful.

5. Have students look at want ads and find ones in which the knowledge of languages is called for or desirable. Have students list and classify such jobs.

6. Have students write to airports, to the World Bank or other international organizations, or to large international business firms in order to find out how knowledge of languages is important.

Figure 2

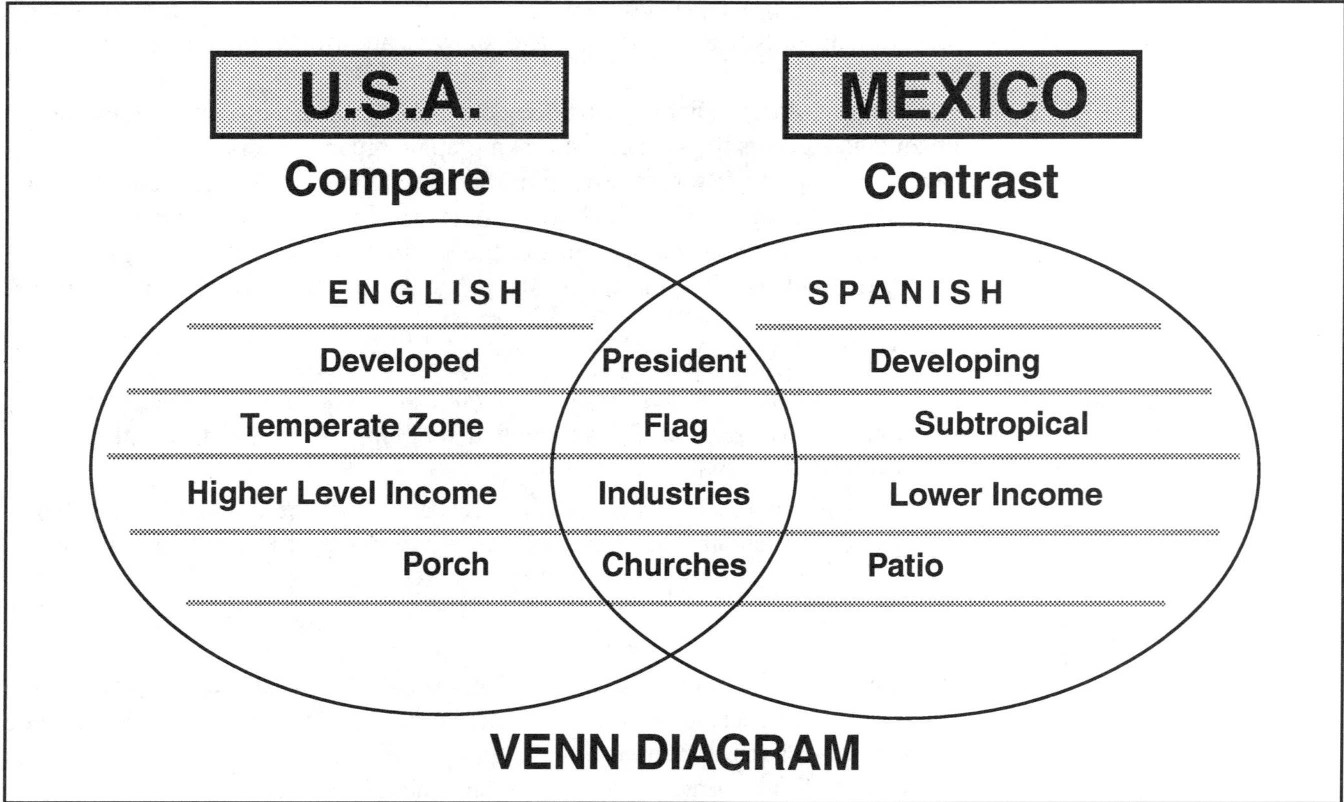

Figure 3

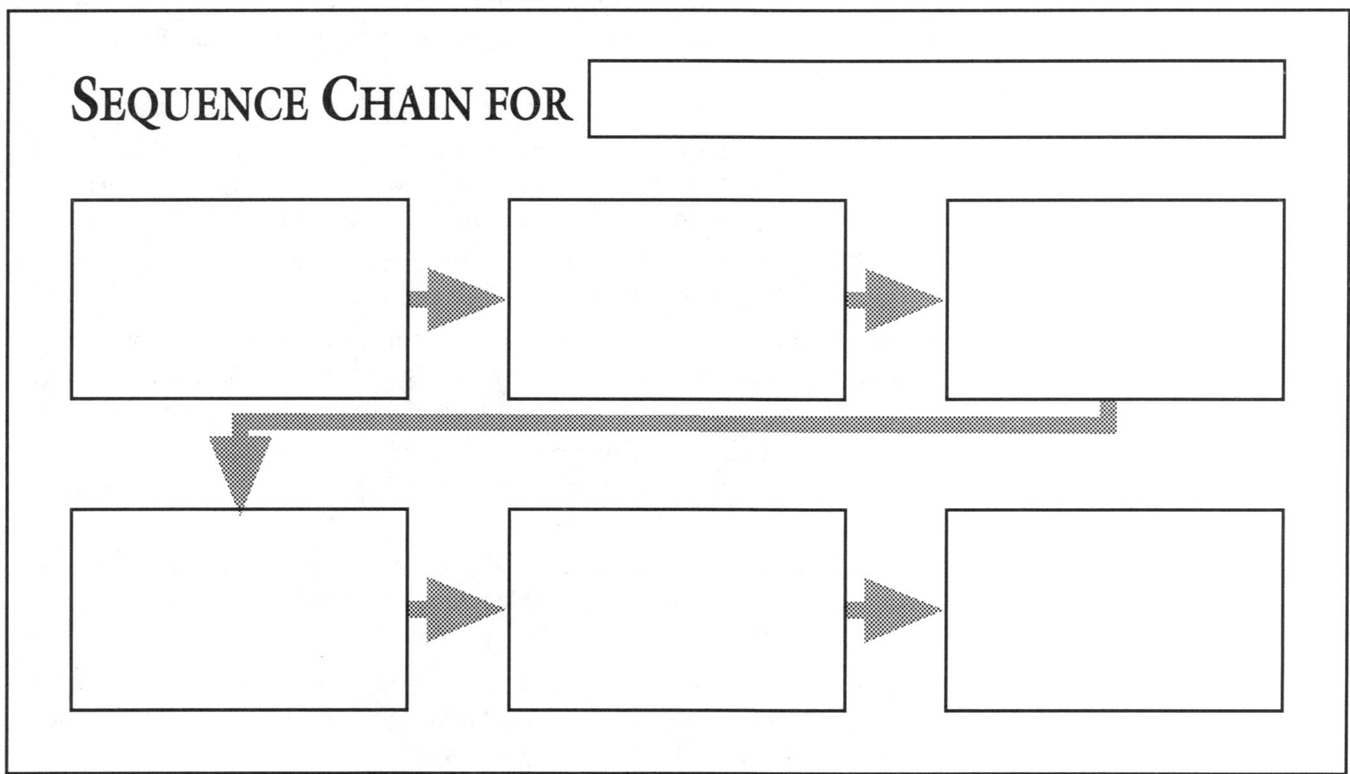

Related References

Careers for Foreign Language Aficionados and Other Multilingual Types, by Ned Seelye, National Textbook, 1992.

Opportunities in Foreign Language Careers, by Wilga Rivers, National Textbook, 1993.

GENERAL TEACHER REFERENCE MATERIALS

This list contains materials useful for the foreign language exploratory teacher. For specific materials for teaching individual chapters, refer to the lists of Resource Materials in the Teaching the Chapters section (there is one list for each chapter). For a list of addresses of publishers, refer to Appendix A, Master Address List. Note: *Educational Leadership* is published by the Association for Supervision and Curriculum Development.

Awareness of Language Series, by Eric Hawkins, Cambridge University Press, 1987.

Complete Guide to Exploratory Foreign Language Programs, by Dora F. Kennedy and William E. De Lorenzo, National Textbook, 1985.

Cooperative Learning Resources for Teachers, by Spencer Kagan. Resources for Teachers, 1989. (Can be obtained by writing Suite 201, 2704 Camino Capistrano, Laguna Miguel, CA 92677)

"Creating Tests Worth Taking," by Grant Wiggin, *Educational Leadership*, May 1992, pp. 26-33.

Culturally Responsive Teaching, by Ana Maria Vinegas, Educational Testing Service, Princeton, NJ, 1991.

"The Curriculum and Cultural Diversity," by Margaret Wilkenson, *Academic Connections*, College Board, Summer 1989.

"Exploratory Foreign Language Courses in the Middle or Junior High School," by Dora F. Kennedy. ERIC Digest. September 1985. Center for Applied Linguistics.

"How to Observe Cooperative Learning Groups," by Carol Furtwengler, *Educational Leadership,* April 1992, pp. 59-62. (Contains a chart of cooperative learning models)

"Global Education," *Educational Leadership,* April 1991. (Entire issue)

"Language Learning Strategies," by Rebecca Oxford et al., *Foreign Language Annals,* February 1991, pp. 29-39.

Languages and Children—Making the Match, by Helena A. Curtain and C. Ann Pesola, Addison-Wesley, 1988.

Learning about Languages, by Elaine A. Lubiner, National Textbook, 1992.

"Learning Styles and the Brain," *Educational Leadership,* October 1990.

Look, Listen, and Learn, by Thomas Alsop, J. Weston Walch. (Activity sheets to help teachers plan for the use of films and videos)

"Multicultural Context: A Key Factor in Teaching," by Sharon Nelson-Barber and Terry Meier, *Academic Connections*, College Board, Spring 1990.

"Teaching Thinking," by Scott Willis, *Curriculum Update*, Association for Supervision and Curriculum Development, June 1992.

Tips for Foreign Language Teachers Who Can't Sing or Dance, by Caroline Marion, J. Weston Walch, 1983.

Webster's New World Dictionary, Student edition. Prentice-Hall.

"Whose Culture?" *Educational Leadership,* December 1991/January 1992. (Entire issue devoted to multicultural education)

Word Origins and Their Romantic Stories, by Wilfred Funk, Bell Publishers (Division of Crown Books), 1978. (Available through Publishers Central Bureau, Avenel, NJ 07001)

Other Resources

Global Language Camps, Inc., Route 4, Box 330-A, Slatesville, NC 28677. (For information on Camp Espérance and Camp Esperanza Summer Immersion Camps)

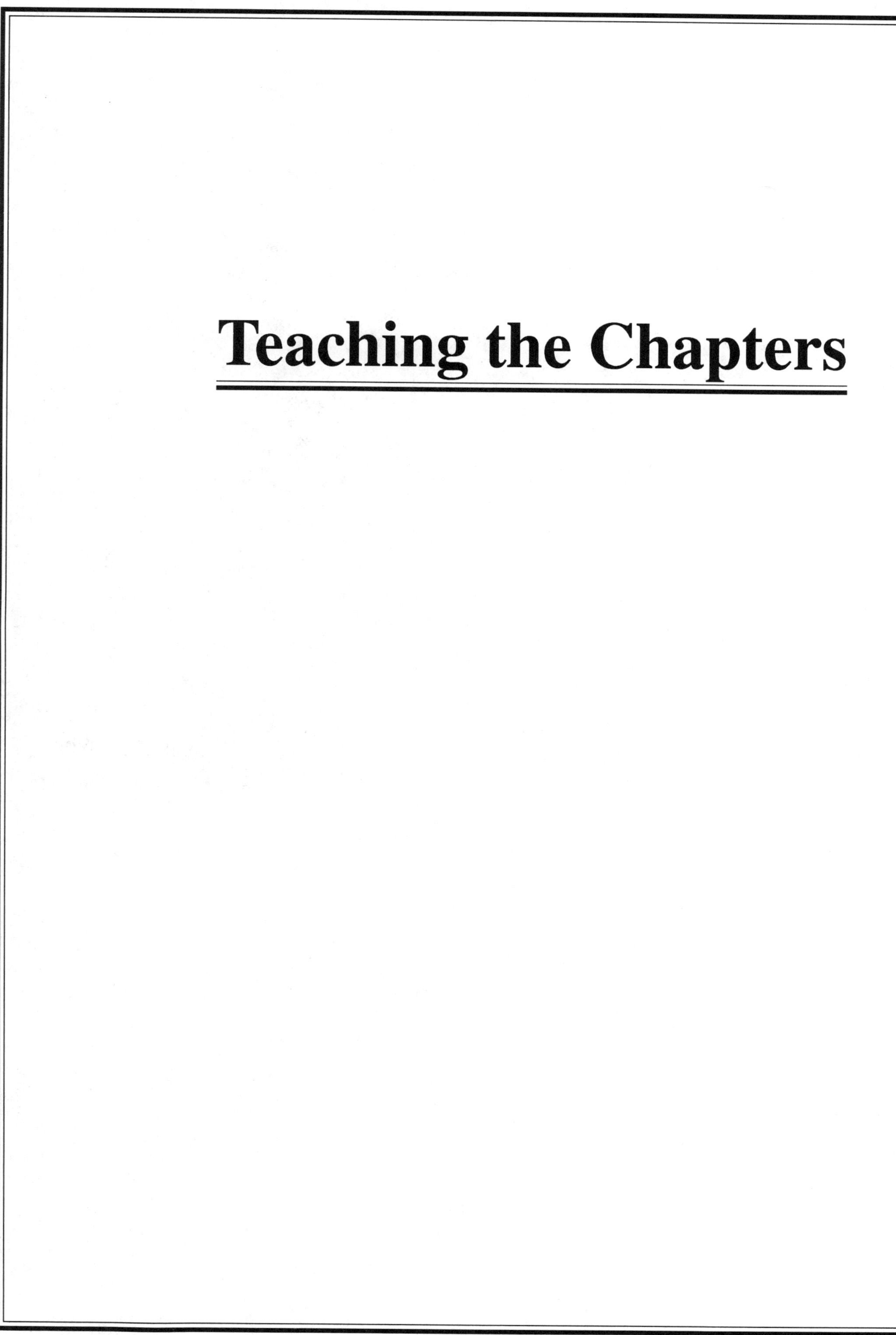

Teaching the Chapters

CHAPTER 1
COMMUNICATING FOR WORLD UNDERSTANDING

Goal

To introduce students to the concept of the nature of language as communication; to help students acquire a global view through awareness of the world's languages; to introduce students to the value of learning foreign languages

Objectives/Outcomes

After working with this chapter, students should be able to:

1. Understand the nature of language in communication
2. Show awareness of the vast array of the world's languages and to recognize some words in a few, e.g., Spanish, French, German
3. Describe forms of communication that don't use words
4. Explain how new words are constantly being added to languages
5. Show awareness of the role that foreign language skills can play in their future careers

Testing for the chapter should be based on these outcomes. (See Assessment in the Methodology section of this manual.)

Implementing the Chapter

As discussed in the Methodology section of this manual, it is recommended that chapter 1 be presented first to launch the foreign language exploratory course, even though the text need not be used sequentially. In fact, it is recommended that the first four chapters be used simultaneously with work on the individual languages in part 2 of the book. See pages 9 and 10 for introducing students to the FLEX program and for a suggested lesson plan for daily lessons.

Preparation

1. To introduce students to the chapter (and to the FLEX course in general), the classroom should be decorated with posters of different countries (often obtainable from airlines). A general map of the world or a map showing the world's languages should be displayed. A variety of flags could be used to decorate the room. Common greetings in different languages in large letters or symbols could appear around the classroom. Include a few English words derived from other languages. There could be an "Exploratory Island," with authentic cultural materials from different countries. (Be sure to avoid stereotypical visuals.)

2. If you are launching the FLEX course with chapter 1, include these activities:

   a. Explain how the course will work, what is expected. Hand out a letter for parents (signed by the principal), explaining the nature and value of a foreign language exploratory program.

   b. Have students complete the pretest (see Appendix B). Explain that the test will not be graded. Tell students that at the end of the course they will take another test like it to compare their answers. (In the spirit of an exploratory course, have students review the prefixes *pre-* and *post-* at this point.) Students could work in groups of four to do the test; however, collect a copy from each student.

   c. Teach one or two greetings from the chapter for the language that is going to be explored first.

3. *Warm-up.* Here are a number of launchers for the chapter. They would be appropriate for the first day of a foreign language exploratory course.

   • Have a class discussion about different languages and where they are spoken (including those spoken in the United States).

   • Use an activity or game in which students identify the materials displayed around the room.

   • Ask students who know a greeting in another language to teach it to the class.

Presentation

Have students read sections of the chapter independently or as a shared reading. Assign the following tasks as cooperative pair work:

1. *How We Communicate* section: Have students illustrate one of the communication systems mentioned and orally describe how it works.

2. *Language Sounds Have Meanings* section: Have students write ten words they know from other languages and indicate the language of each.

3. *Words, Words, Words* section: Have students describe the dictionary they use and write down the various parts of a dictionary entry: e.g., pronunciation, meaning, origin of the word, other forms of the word.

4. *Why Study Other Languages* section: Have students choose five jobs on the chart and explain how knowing a foreign language could be useful in each job.

Additional/Follow-up Activities

1. *Class project.* Have students make a "dictionary in process." Cover a bulletin board with white paper. Invite students to write any new words they have learned (regardless of language). They must give the meaning and the language of origin. Make students responsible for copying what is written and changing the paper when the bulletin board is full. A class dictionary can then be published from what is recorded.

2. *Small-group project.* Have students create a poster showing some form of communication, for example, lines from a computer program, road signs. Students can present posters to classmates who determine what each poster is communicating.

3. *Poems.* Read Lewis Carroll's poem "Jabberwocky." Have students write "Jabberwocky" poems using made-up words of their own.

4. *New words.* The New Webster's College Dictionary published by Random House in 1991 had the following new entries:

   garbology, loony tunes, laptop, infomercial, glasnost (from Russian, referring to a more democratic government), *karaoke* (from Japanese, informal singing by patrons in a restaurant)

Have students find out the meanings of these new words and include as many as they can in a short story.

5. *Slang.* Slang is informal language, and many new words that enter the language are slang. Have students list new "slang" words that they use in their speech.

6. *Career-related activities.* Do activities described in the Introduction, page 21.

Answer Key

page 3
Hellos: Pronunciations
Spanish: ¡Hola! (*o* la)
Russian: Привет!   (pree*vyet*)
Latin: Salve (*sal* way)
German: Guten Tag (*gooten* tahk)
French: Bonjour (bo *zhoor*) (first *o* = nasal vowel)
Italian: Ciao (chow)
Japanese: こんにちは。   (koneechee wah)

page 4
¿Dónde está el teléfono?: Where is the phone?
Tengo que llamar a mi mamá.: I have to call my mother.

Activity 1
• Language involves *communication.*
• Language sounds must have *meaning.*
• A way of communicating without words is using *gestures.*
The picture shows a lighthouse. It communicates through light signals. The message tells ships about dangerous conditions on the ocean or sea.

Supplementary Information

I. Languages of the World

The languages of the world with the largest number of speakers are Chinese, English, Hindi, Spanish, Russian, and Arabic. Information about these languages and the countries in which they are spoken can be found in general almanacs.

II. Ethnic Groups in the United States

The multicultural and multiracial makeup of the United States is documented in the 1990 Census Report as follows: white, 80.3%; African American, 12%; Hispanic, 9%; Asian, 3%; Native American, .8%. Countries from which many recent immigrants have come are the Philippines, Vietnam, Mexico, China, and Korea.

Resource Materials

Note: For addresses of publishers and distributors, refer to Appendix A, Master Address List.

Teacher Reference

Complete Guide to Exploratory Foreign Language Programs, by Dora Kennedy and William De Lorenzo, National Textbook, 1985.

Global Education: From Thought to Action, Association for Supervision and Curriculum Development, 1991.

Multicultural Phrase Book, National Textbook.

The Science of Words, by George A. Muller, Scientific American Library, W. H. Freeman, 1991.

Teaching Culture, by H. Ned Seelye, National Textbook, 1993. (Revised edition)

Class Materials

I. Audiovisual Materials

Speaking of Language, Guidance Associates. (Audiocassette/filmstrip)

Your Career and Foreign Languages, Gessler Publishing. (Audiocassette/filmstrip)

II. Posters/Calendars

Cultural and Festive Days of the World, Available from Educational Extension Systems. (Poster)

Foreign Language Careers, J. Weston Walch. (Posters)

A calendar on American ethnic cultures is available from Educational Extension Systems.

Posters are available from the Northeast Conference on Teaching Foreign Languages.

III. Realia

Flags, pins from numerous countries are available from Claudia's Caravan, National Textbook, and World Press.

IV. Language Development Materials

Learning about Languages, by Elaine Lubiner, National Textbook, 1992.

What's in a Word, by David Zaslow, Good Apple, Inc., 1983. (Hands-on activities dealing with word origins)

V. Games/Puzzles

Global Futures Game. Available from Social Studies School Service.

Where in the World? Available from World Awareness. (Geography game)

Where in the World Is Carmen Sandiego? Puzzle available from Donovan Music and Toy Company. Software available from Social Studies School Service.

VI. Background Reading

Communication Satellites, by D. J. Herda, Franklin Watts, 1988.

Learning about Peoples and Cultures, McDougal, Littell, 1989.

Mercury's Web: The Story of Telecommunications, by Jespersen Randolph and Fritz Randolph, Atheneum, 1981.

Opportunities in Foreign Language Careers, by Wilga Rivers, National Textbook, 1993.

Origins of Language, by L. J. Ludovici. G. P. Putnam's, 1965.

Sign Language, by L. Green and E. Dicker, Franklin Watts, 1981. (Includes a discussion of American Sign Language)

The Story of the Dictionary, by Robert Kraske, Harcourt, Brace, Jovanovich, 1975.

Telecommunications, by John Stevenson, Silver Burdett, 1985.

You Don't Say, by Vernon Pizer, G. P. Putnam's, 1978. (About how people communicate without speech)

Where in the World Is Carmen Sandiego?, Western Publishing, 1991. (Book based on the PBS series/software game)

Wonders of Speech, by Alvin and Virginia Silverstein, Morrow, 1988.

CHAPTER 2
SIGNS AND SYMBOLS, INCLUDING ESPERANTO

Goal

To help students understand the nature of signs and symbols and the role they play all over the world and to familiarize the students with the invented language of Esperanto

Objectives/Outcomes

After working with this chapter, students should be able to:

1. Show awareness of the variety of commonly used signs and symbols and how they convey meaning
2. Recognize a number of common signs and symbols (e.g., dollar sign, musical symbols, international street signs)
3. Discuss the increasing need for signs and symbols as more people travel to countries whose languages they do not know
4. Describe American Sign Language and how it operates in simple terms
5. Explain how symbols can be used to communicate words and sentences, using the examples of ham radio and Morse code
6. Describe the history and nature of one invented language, Esperanto
7. Speak, read, and write the basic greetings in Esperanto found in the chapter
8. Create a sign or symbol to convey a concept

Testing for the chapter should be based on these outcomes. (See Assessment in the Methodology section of this manual.)

Implementing the Chapter

In order to preserve the basic lesson format, which calls for daily foreign language practice during part of the class period, this chapter should be presented with one of the language chapters in part 2.

Preparation

1. *Warm-up.* Have students list the signs and symbols they have seen or encountered in the past week. Point out that signs or symbols communicate an idea without words, often through a pictorial image.

2. If your school has a crest or symbol, discuss its significance with students.

3. Direct students to come prepared to describe (draw on board) or to show an example of a sign or symbol. It could be from a text, newspaper, magazine, etc.

Presentation

1. Have students read the first part of the chapter on signs. List or show some symbols discussed. Have students identify each as fully as they can. Have students present the symbol they have found (see number 3 above).

2. After students read the sections on sign language, ham radio, and Morse Code, have them prepare a simple message to present to the class that is in a code. They should provide a key for understanding the code. (Students using Morse Code or the International Radio Alphabet can refer other students to the text to decipher their message.)

3. Conduct a brainstorming session in which the class lists additional symbols, signs, or symbol systems not discussed in the chapter. *Examples:* barber pole, map symbols, punctuation marks, Boy Scout semaphore system, heraldry, symbols of political parties, hex signs (Pennsylvania Dutch), Olympic symbol.

4. Prepare an activity sheet with questions about Esperanto that students can answer by reading the text. Sample questions: How old is Esperanto? Where does the name Esperanto come from? After students read the section on Esperanto, have them complete the sheet and discuss their answers.

5. Have an Esperanto Information Blitz. Use information obtained from sources mentioned in the text or at the end of this chapter, or from the library. Each student is given material and must explain its contents to the class in the "information blitz."

6. Have students discuss these questions in small groups and then present their answers to the class: Why is Esperanto different from other languages? How is it like other languages?

Additional/Follow-up Activities

1. *Class project.* The class can develop a booklet listing any signs and symbols around the school and immediate neighborhood. It could be published and given to new students, including students from other countries, to be used as an aid in getting around.

2. *Braille and sign language.* Assign half the class to investigate Braille and the other half to investigate American Sign Language. Organize each group so that there is a system of reporting and a series of brief demonstrations.

3. *Important inventions.* Have students investigate the history of Samuel F. B. Morse's invention of the telegraph and of Marconi's experiments that led to the radio.

4. *Icons.* Some computer programs make use of symbols to communicate. These are generally called *icons*. Students who are computer buffs can prepare a demonstration showing some of these symbols and explaining what they mean. Have students investigate the origin and history of the word *icon*.

5. *Seals.* Have students write to the state governor's office to obtain a copy of the state seal, flag, motto, etc. Have students report on the information they obtain.

6. *Insignia.* Have students prepare a report on the insignia of the various armed services or on the logos of different groups.

7. *Presenting an Esperanto dialogue.* Have students work on the Esperanto dialogue and present it to foreign language classes (without telling what language the dialogue is in). Have students report back on the experience, for example, explaining which classes could best understand the dialogue.

8. *Songs in Esperanto.* Have students do further work on Esperanto. Obtain a song tape from the Esperanto League for North America such as *Sing Esperanto with Janice and John* (see Resource Materials) and have students try to determine what is being said. Obtain a book on Esperanto or at least an Esperanto/English dictionary for students to examine. Have them list words in Esperanto that are similar to ones in English.

Answer Key

page 11
− subtraction, + addition, × multiplication, ÷ division, % percent, < less than, > greater than

page 12
Activity 2
B. symbol used to indicate "handicapped," often to designate a special access area or a reserved parking place for persons with disabilities
atom symbol
mortar and pestle: symbol of pharmacists, sometimes found on drug store signs. They are utensils used to crush material into powder.
treble clef (musical notation)

page 16
Mystery Word: Mayday means "help me." It is a term used by all nations to call for help on the high seas. It comes from the French *m'aider,* which literally means "help me."

Supplementary Information

I. Ham Radio

Amateur radio began during the early 1900s when the Italian inventor Marconi transmitted radio signals. In 1919, a ham operator used his signal to broadcast recorded music to people in his area. They received the music on crystal sets. Events like this led to the development of commercial radio. Have interested students investigate the early history of radio.

II. World Esperanto Headquarters

The Universal Esperanto Association (U.E.A.) is located in Rotterdam, Netherlands. There are branches in large cities throughout the world. The U.E.A. sponsors the annual World Congress on Esperanto, held in a different city each year. Delegates from over seventy countries attend.

III. Invented Languages

Esperanto is just one of the invented languages, although it has taken more hold than others. One of these languages is *Loglan*, which stands for logical language. It was developed by James Cooke Brown in the 1950s. For more information on this language, see *Scientific American*, June 1960.

Resource Materials

Note: For addresses of publishers and distributors, refer to Appendix A, Master Address List.

Class Materials: Signs and Symbols

I. Films/Videotapes

Beginning Reading and Sign Language, Aylmer Press, 1991. (Video)
The Miracle Worker. (Film tells the story of Helen Keller and her teacher Anne Sullivan)
Say It by Signing, Random House. (Video)
Sign Me a Story, Random House. (Video)

II. Language Materials

The following materials show signs and symbols used in different countries.
French Sign Language, National Textbook.
German Sign Language, National Textbook.
Italian Sign Language, National Textbook.
Spanish Sign Language, National Textbook.

III. Books

Heels, Wheels, and Wire, by F. Rogers and A. Beard, J. B. Lippincott, 1967. (Story of messages and symbols)
Morse, Marconi, and You, by Irwin Math, Charles Scribner's, 1979.
Symbols and Their Meaning, by Rolf Myller, Atheneum, 1978.

Teacher Reference: Esperanto

Jen Nia Mondo (Here Is Our World), Audio Forum. (A short study of Esperanto, with a tape)
"On the Acquisition of Esperanto," by Dan Maxwell, *Studies in Second Language Acquisition*, February 1988, pp. 51-61.
Teach Yourself Esperanto, by John Cresswell and John Hartley, 1988.

Class Materials: Esperanto

I. Song/Tapes

Sing Esperanto with Janice and John, by Charlotte Kohrs and Janice and John Atkinson, Esperanto League for North America, 1987. (Twelve songs for children and beginning students of Esperanto)

Song Festival, by Marta Evans, Esperanto League for North America, 1982.

II. Magazines

Magazine published by Children around the World. (See Useful Addresses below.)

Juna Amiko (Young Friend), Esperanto League for North America.

III. Dictionaries

Esperanto Dictionary, Esperanto League for North America, 1984. (Includes Esperanto-English, English-Esperanto listings)

Practical Picture Dictionary of Esperanto, Esperanto League for North America, 1979.

IV. Books

Is That Our Mother in the Bottle?, by Jessica Davidson, Franklin Watts, 1972. (Includes a discussion of Esperanto)

Languages of the World, by Kenneth Katzner, Routledge, 1986. (Includes a discussion of Esperanto)

Zamenhof, Creator of Esperanto, Esperanto League for North America, 1980.

Useful Addresses

Signs and Symbols

    Gallaudet University
    800 Florida Ave., NE
    Washington, D.C. 20002
    (A source for information on sign language and topics relating to communication by the deaf)

    Network QSL Cards
    P.O. Box 19200
    Alexandria, Louisiana 71315
    (Sample QSL cards can be obtained from this address.)

Esperanto

    American Association of Teachers of Esperanto
    5140 San Lorenzo Dr.
    Santa Barbara, CA 93511

    Children around the World
    (Infanoj Cirkaŭ La Mondo)
    3876 Belmont Ave.
    San Diego, CA 92116
    (Publishes a children's magazine and other materials on Esperanto including a booklet on geography *Ni Esploru La Mondon, We Explore the World*)

Esperanto League for North America (ELNA)
P.O. Box 1129
El Cerrito, CA 94530
(Main source for information on Esperanto. Provides a guide for teaching Esperanto that includes a list of resources, which can be obtained on request)

CHAPTER 3
YOUR LANGUAGE AND MINE
AND HOW IT CAME TO BE

Goal

To give students an understanding of the story of the English language, demonstrating that many elements of English came from other languages; to show students how a language changes over time; to help students appreciate the rich, multicultural nature of the United States as reflected in its place names

Objectives/Outcomes

After working with this chapter, students should be able to:

1. Describe the main historical events that shaped the English language
2. List the peoples and languages that contributed directly to the development of English
3. Explain the origins of a number of English words derived from other languages
4. Define basic terms used in the chapter and explain their significance, including *Indo-European, Angles, Saxons, Normans, B.C., A.D., derivatives, standardized*
5. Show understanding that languages keep changing
6. Explain the origins of Native American, French, Spanish, and English-derived place names in the United States, as described in the chapter
7. Demonstrate knowledge of the origin of place names in their own area

Testing for the chapter should be based on these outcomes. (See Assessment in the Methodology section of this manual.)

Implementing the Chapter

In order to preserve the basic lesson format, which calls for daily foreign language practice during part of the class period, this chapter should be presented with one of the language chapters in part 2.

Preparation

1. For the first part of the chapter, have displayed a large map that shows England, Scandinavia, northern Germany, and France so that students can locate the main events reported in the chapter. For the second part of the chapter, on place names in the United States, have displayed a large wall map of the United States showing state boundaries. Stress geography skills as students work in the chapter and make presentations.

2. *Warm-up.* Prepare a transparency with sentences in Anglo-Saxon, Middle English (the language of Chaucer), and in the language of Shakespeare. (These are typically available in books on the history of English.) Ask students to try to read the sentences. Then point out that all the sentences are in a "form" of English, out of which our current language developed. Lead students to conclude that English has changed over the centuries. Tell them that in the chapter they will find out why.

3. Show a filmstrip or video on the history of English (for example, the video *The Story of English*—see Resource Materials) or ones on medieval England.

Presentation

1. As one procedure, the sections on the history of English can be assigned as a shared reading. As students complete reading each scene, assist them in tracing the events and movements of people on a map in the classroom. Have students work in groups to prepare a map that shows the movement of people into England and time periods in which the movements occurred.

2. The first sections in the chapter, the scenes from the history of English, lend themselves to dramatization. Assign them to different groups of students to dramatize. Each group would be responsible for presenting a part of the drama "The Story of English." Encourage students to do more research to add to the information they have learned in the chapter. Have students prepare written summaries of what they have presented.

3. For the second section of the chapter, on place names, divide the class into groups of four. Assign different parts of the section to different groups. Each group refers to the wall map of the United States to locate each place that is named. At a designated time, the groups report to one another: students from the group read their passage aloud while one member of the team points to the places mentioned on the wall map.

4. As a review of place names, make a list of at least fifteen place names in the chapter. Have a "Place Name Bee." Divide the class into two groups. To score a point, a team must give the meaning and location of each place you mention. The losing team must prepare a list with the correct answers.

5. Once students have read the chapter, have them discuss these questions: How has English changed over the centuries? What caused the changes? How were places in the United States named?

   Point out that they are drawing conclusions from what they have learned.

Additional/Follow-up Activities

1. *"Language Connection" dictionaries.* Have students prepare "Language Connection" dictionaries. In the dictionaries, students list English words, showing their derivation and meaning. Some students may want to illustrate their dictionary. If students have or are studying one of the languages in part 2 of the text, they may choose to focus on words that came into English from that language. To complete the task, students should refer to large, unabridged English dictionaries that give word origins. (They should be taught the term *unabridged*.)

2. *Shakespeare's English.* Show several lines from one of Shakespeare's plays on a transparency. Have students attempt to "translate" the lines into modern English. Reiterate the concept that language does not remain static. Have students research some information about Shakespeare: when he lived, the titles of some his plays, the theaters of his time, and related topics.

3. *English around the world.* Point out that English is the second most widely spoken world language, after Chinese. Have students prepare a report listing the countries in which English is spoken.

4. *Rap songs.* Have student teams develop rap songs conveying information they have learned in the chapter. They can use the rap song at the end of the chapter in the text as a model. The songs can be published as a class booklet, with each student autographing his/her song.

5. *Native American names.* Distribute 8 1/2" by 11" blank maps of the United States. Have students fill in the maps with place names derived from Native Americans, giving the meaning of each name: e.g., *Niagara,* "thundering water."

6. *A guided tour.* The class plans a tour of places mentioned or shown in the chapter. The class is divided into teams, and each team is assigned a section of the chapter to prepare. Each team presents its report as a guided tour. The "guides" describe the places being visited and may use visuals.

Answer Key

page 25
London is on the Thames River.

page 29
Activity 5
- The Germanic goddess of spring was *Eastre*, after whom Easter was named.

- *Saturday* was named after *Saturn,* the ancient Roman god of agriculture and harvest. Saturn is also the name of a planet.

Activity 6
sky, skill, scare, reindeer, skin, window

page 35
Mardi Gras is the day before the Christian season of Lent, the 40-day period before Easter, when Christians fast and do penance.

page 39
William Shakespeare; some plays: *Romeo and Juliet, Macbeth, Hamlet*

Supplementary Information

I. The Periods of English

All living languages constantly change and have a history. In the year 1500 English had approximately 70,000 words. It now has over 600,000. The history of English is divided into several periods. The Old English period (from about 450 to 1066 A.D.) is the age of the Angles and the Saxons, when the language had its beginnings. The Middle English period (from 1066 to 1500) occurred after the Norman Conquest and is the period in which French greatly influenced English. The Modern Period (after 1500) is the period in which we live. Books on the history of English will have samples of English at different periods in history. You might want to point out these historical divisions to students, particularly since students may see references to them in large dictionaries as they look up etymologies. In many dictionaries, O.E. refers to "Old English"; M.E. refers to "Middle English."

II. Native American Languages

Some sources state that there were over 2,000 Native American languages when Columbus first arrived. Most of these are no longer spoken.

English has been enriched by many Native American words and expressions. Here are some examples: moccasin, papoose, pow-wow, tepee, wigwam, wampum, squaw, tomahawk, skunk, chipmunk, opossum, hickory, squash. You might want to incorporate these words into a game.

One of the Native American languages that has recently caught attention is *Lakota*, the language spoken by a branch of the Sioux Indians of the Plains. This language was featured in the film *Dances with Wolves.* Example of a *Lakota* word: *T'at'aka*, which is pronounced "tah *t'awn* caw" and which means buffalo.

III. Dialects

American English has a number of regional and cultural dialects, as does English spoken in other countries. Students should be briefly introduced to the concept of language variations called *dialects*. This should be done with sensitivity and without stereotyping. The following concepts should be emphasized:

a. There are language variations in all countries. Usually one of the dialects becomes standard.

b. English is spoken differently in the various countries where it is the official language (including variations in vocabulary).

IV. Place Names

Here are a few state nicknames or explanations of name origins. They could be incorporated into a class activity or game. (1) A native word for homeland—Hawaii, (2) Spanish for "snowclad"—Nevada, (3) Russian version of an Eskimo word— Alaska, (4) Sunflower State—Kansas, (5) Blue Grass State—Kentucky, (6) Lone Star State—Texas, (7) Golden State—California, (8) Buckeye State—Ohio, (9) Green Mountain State—Vermont, (10) Hoosier—Indiana.

Resource Materials

Note: For addresses of publishers and distributors, refer to Appendix A, Master Address List.

Teacher Reference

The Discovery of America, by Renardo Barden, Greenhaven Press, 1989.

History of English in Its Own Words, by Craig M. Carver, HarperCollins, 1991.

State Names, Seals, Flags, and Symbols, by Benjamin and Barbara Sheurer, Greenwood Press, 1987.

The Story of English, by Robert McCrum, William Cran, and Robert MacNeil, Penguin Books, 1986. (For examples of English through the centuries)

Word Origins and Their Romantic Stories, by Wilfred Funk, Bell Publishers (Division of Crown), 1978. (Available through Publishers Central Bureau, Avenel, NJ 07001)

Class Materials

I. Videos/Filmstrips

The Story of English, available from EMC Publishing. (This is the PBS series that aired in 1986, hosted by Robert MacNeil.)

II. Posters

History of English, J. Weston Walch

III. Background Reading

Ancient Indians: The First Americans, by Ray Gallant, Enslow Publishers, 1989.

Awareness of Language (Exploration Series), Eric Hawkins, Cambridge University Press. The following 32-page booklets:

Get the Message, by Helen Astley. (On body language)

How Language Works, by Barry Jones. (On discovering the nature of language)

Languages Varieties and Change, by Cathy Pomphrey. (On languages of the world and how they are related)

Spoken and Written Language, Eric Hawkins. (On English spelling and other alphabets)

Conquistadores, by Meridel LeSueur, Franklin Watts, 1973.

English from the Roots Up, Joegil Lundquist, American Classical League (no date).

The French Explorers in America, by Walter Bucker, Longman, 1961.

Indians: An Activity Book, by John Artman, Good Apple, 1981.

"Thor, Thunder, and Thursday," Ray Walker, *Highlights for Children Magazine*, Resource Index Issue, 1982. (Mythology surrounding English names for days of the week)

What's in a Word?, David Zaslow, Good Apple, Inc., 1983. (Hands-on activities dealing with word origins)

Useful Addresses

American Classical League Service Bureau
Miami University
Oxford, OH 45056
(Posters of derivatives)

British Tourist Agency
40 West Fifty-Seventh St.
New York, NY 10019
(For information about Great Britain and photographs of famous landmarks)

Dakota Indian Foundation
201 South Main Street
Chamberlain, SD 57325
(For information on Native Americans of the Plains)

CHAPTER 4
FAMILIES OF LANGUAGES: THEIR SIMILARITIES AND DIFFERENCES

Goal

To help students learn that the languages of the world are grouped into different families and that there are many similarities among languages in the same family

Objectives/Outcomes

After working with the chapter, students should be able to:

1. Show understanding of the concept of language families
2. Name the major branches and languages of the Indo-European family
3. Name at least two additional language families and one or two member languages
4. Show awareness that there are several alphabets and name languages that use alphabets other than the Roman
5. Explain at a simple level how languages of the same family are alike
6. Explain why English is in the Germanic branch of the Indo-European family

   Testing for the chapter should be based on these outcomes. (See Assessment in the Methodology section of this manual.)

Implementing the Chapter

In order to preserve the basic lesson format, which calls for daily foreign language practice during part of the class period, this chapter should be presented with one of the language chapters in part 2.

Preparation

1. Obtain a wall map showing languages of the world, if possible, to encourage discussion and give students a frame of reference.
2. *Warm-up.* Point out to students that just as scientists classify plants and animals based on certain characteristics, scientists of language (called linguists) classify languages. Tell them that there still are mysteries about languages that linguists are trying to solve. Encourage students to speculate how languages can be alike (words can be the same, they may come from the same language—e.g., Spanish, French from Latin—etc.).

Presentation

1. For this chapter, the class will use their language detective skills. Give each student a list of languages, including ones that are less common. Students are to choose a given number to investigate and determine the family for each language and where the language is spoken. Students are to incorporate their research into a written report. Investigation may be conducted through cooperative learning groups. (Encyclopedias generally give this information, often under the entries "Language" or "Language

Families." Dictionaries also are useful. Make sure that these resources are available.) On the day designated for reports, the presentation may take the form of a news conference format, in which "panels of experts" are interviewed by "inquiring reporters." Reporters are to prepare questions ahead of time.

2. Have students read the chapter. Each student selects the most interesting page to share with the class. Students should explain why they found that particular page interesting.

Additional/Follow-up Activities

1. *Class project.* Have the class create a bulletin board display: a table of major world languages or maps showing where languages are spoken.

2. *Compare and contrast.* Have students prepare a Venn diagram (see pages 21 and 22), comparing the Roman and Greek alphabets. Students can refer to chapter 16 for the ancient Greek alphabet.

3. *German and English connections.* Have students list words of Germanic origin in English, adding to the list of similar words in the text. Students should be encouraged to use a variety of research techniques, such as looking at a English-language dictionary that shows word origins, interviewing a German speaker or teacher, looking at a German textbook.

4. *World language project.* Have students work cooperatively to prepare a booklet of "world languages." They decide on contents for each language, such as where the language is spoken, number of speakers, alphabet used, several words from the language, three important facts about the language, etc. They assign tasks so that a number of languages are covered.

Answer Key

page 44
Activity 2
Possible answers: *Roman alphabet*: Latin, French, English; *Greek alphabet:* Greek; *Cyrillic alphabet:* Russian, Bulgarian.

page 46
Activities and Projects
2. Definitions of the Mystery Words:

pidgin: a mixed language put together for practical communication among people who do not know one another's languages. It is usually a simplified form of one of the languages. Example is *pidgin English*, used principally for business and trade purposes in parts of the Pacific such as New Guinea and in West Africa. The origin of the word *pidgin* is not precisely known. It is thought to have developed from the Chinese pronunciation of the English word *business*.

creole: a pidgin language that has become the native language of a group of people through enriched vocabulary and additional forms. The word is from Spanish *criollo*, a person of Spanish descent born in the "New World" during the discovery and exploration period. Some examples of areas where creole is spoken are Haiti, Jamaica, Surinam, and Brazil.

Supplementary Information

I. The Sea Island Gullahs

The Sea Islands lie off the coast of South Carolina and Georgia. Gullah is the name for the creole language spoken on them. Creole is the name for a mixed language put together by people who don't know one another's language. Gullah consists of English words mixed with words from languages of West Africa. In investigating the speech of Sea Islanders, linguists have concluded that it reflects the languages of the many areas of Africa whose inhabitants were brought over as slaves in the early 1700s: the languages include Yoruba, Hausa, Ibo, Ewe. Among the investigators has been Dr. Lorenzo Turner, an African American linguist knowledgeable about African languages. Even though the Sea Island people have resided on the islands for over 300 years, they have retained many African elements in their spoken English because of having little contact with the mainland. Some African words in Gullah have been passed on to English, such as *goober* for "peanut" and *voodoo* for "witchcraft." Scholars continue to study these fascinating residents and their language. More information is available from the Center for Urban Ethnography, University of Pennsylvania, Philadelphia, PA.

II. The Mother Language

Linguists at the University of Michigan are attempting to find the mother tongue from which all other languages were eventually derived. One language sleuth states that there are about 5,000 languages, but all of them can be traced to six or seven *superfamilies*. The researchers are tracking the languages by following the trail of human migration, beginning in Africa and ending with the arrival in the Western Hemisphere of the ancestors of Native Americans about 35,000 years ago. For more information on this topic, refer to the article "Tracking Mother of 5,000 Tongues," in *Insight*, February 5, 1990.

III. Table of Languages

Tables of languages are available in reference books. See, for example, Collier's Encyclopedia, under "Languages of the World."

Resource Materials

Note: For addresses of publishers and distributors, refer to Appendix A, Master Address List.

Class Materials

I. Poster

A "Languages of the World" wall map is available from Rand McNally.

II. Books

Jambo Means Hello, by Muriel Feelings, Dial Press, 1974. (A Swahili alphabet book)

The Languages of the World, by Kenneth Katzner, Routledge, 1989.

Russian Alphabet Book, by Fan Parker, Coward-McCann, 1961.

Useful Addresses

American Classical League Service Bureau
Miami University
Oxford, OH 45056
(For information and posters)

British Tourist Agency
40 West Fifty-Seventh St.
New York, NY 10019
(For information about Great Britain and photographs of famous landmarks)

Dakota Indian Foundation
201 South Main Street
Chamberlain, SD 57325
(For information on Native Americans of the Plains)

Prince George's County Public Schools
American Indian Education Program
7711 Livingston Rd.
Oxon Hill, MD 20745

CHAPTER 5
EXPLORING SPANISH AND THE HISPANIC WORLD

Goal

To introduce students to the Spanish language, to the places where it is spoken, and to Spanish-speaking peoples; to develop students' awareness of the borrowings in English from Spanish; to promote students' appreciation for Hispanic people in the United States

Objectives/Outcomes

After working with this chapter, students should be able to:

1. Understand, say, read, and write the basic Spanish expressions found in the chapter: numbers, telling time, days of the week, months of the year, greetings, classroom vocabulary

2. Recite the Spanish alphabet, understand Spanish pronunciation, and some basic elements of Spanish structure (at the pre-level I stage)

3. Explain the connections between English and Spanish by naming some derivatives and words borrowed from Spanish, as well as some places where Spanish is spoken in the United States

4. Name and locate places in the world where Spanish is spoken

Supplemental Outcomes

1. Give examples of contributions of Hispanic Americans to the culture of the United States

2. Discuss careers in which Spanish language skills would be useful

3. Describe some aspects of Spanish and Hispanic American culture

Testing for the chapter should be based on these outcomes. (See Assessment in the Methodology section of this manual.)

Implementing the Chapter

Preparation

1. Decorate the classroom with materials relating to Hispanic cultures (e.g., travel posters, maps of Spain, Central and South America, and the Caribbean). Have a Spanish corner with books about Hispanic culture and countries, as well as realia. Use recordings of Spanish music for atmosphere.

2. *Warm-up.* Have students take a simulated trip to a Spanish-speaking area. Present a film or video on such an area. Mexico, Puerto Rico, or Spain are most familiar to students. See the Resource Materials at the end of this chapter for a list of videos.

3. Have a class brainstorming activity. Point out that students already know some Spanish words. Elicit words like *adiós, tacos, sombrero, olé.* Write the words on a poster and encourage students to add to the list as they work in the chapter.

Presentation

Teach the language sections concurrently with sections that deal with geography, culture, and other general topics. (See page 10 in the Methodology section on how to organize a class period.)

Each lesson should include a practice segment in the language explored. Refer to Language Learning Strategies and Activities (see pages 11 to 13) to supplement those in the chapter. (It is recommended that the language segment of the period be conducted in Spanish as far as possible.) Refer to the Spanish Pronunciation Guide at the end of the text chapter, if necessary. You might also want to get some simple language learning tapes to check pronunciation (see Resource Materials).

Here are some suggestions for specific sections:

1. In addition to Puerto Rico, other Spanish-speaking islands in the West Indies should be pointed out, such as Cuba and the Dominican Republic.

2. *Telling time.* Have the students make clocks out of paper plates, adding cardboard hands if possible (or drawing in hands). Students exchange clocks and respond to the question "¿Qué hora es?"

3. *Labeling classroom objects.* As students study classroom words, have them put labels on the classroom objects whose names they are learning. As a follow-up, devise a game in which students are given cards with Spanish names, which they must place on the correct objects.

Additional/Follow-up Activities

1. *Reports.* A student or a group chooses a Spanish-speaking country to investigate and produces a written report that includes a map, information on places and customs of the country, pictures, and other interesting facts they discovered. Set standards for the report, such as table of contents, list of references, etc.

2. *Picture dictionary.* Have students produce a dictionary of Spanish words. They might prepare an alphabet book for children, listing and illustrating words that begin with each letter of the Spanish alphabet. Have a Spanish-English dictionary available for student reference. Have students share their work with a first-grade class.

3. *Famous Hispanic Americans.* Have students do library research and identify at least five Hispanic Americans and their contributions to the United States.

4. *Hispanic music.* Encourage students to learn about the music of the Hispanic world, including instruments and dances. Have them report to class, using tapes if possible.

5. *Hispanic folktales.* Hispanic culture is rich in folktales. Have students read one or two independently and share their stories with the class. Enlist the aid of the school librarian.

6. *Spanish around us.* Have students investigate and report on the Hispanic presence in their area, if appropriate.

Answer Key

page 51
Activity 1
Spain and Portugal make up the Iberian peninsula.

page 54
Activity 3
A. Some places in the United States where Spanish is spoken: California, Texas, Florida, New Mexico, New York City, Chicago.

B. 1. California, Colorado, Arizona, Texas, New Mexico   2. Florida
    3. New York, Washington, D.C., San Antonio, Chicago, Los Angeles

page 57
Activity 5
1. ocho   2. sí   3. adiós   4. ¿Cómo se llama?   5. piñata   6. María
7. uno   8. mesa   9. burro   10. San   11. Hasta mañana.

page 59
veinticuatro, veinticinco, veintisiete, veintiocho, veintinueve, treinta

page 60
Activity 6
A. 1. cincuenta   2. doce   3. siete   4. cincuenta   5. (Answers will vary.)
6. diez   7. sesenta   8. (Answers will vary.)   9. veintinueve

Mystery Word
perritos calientes: hotdogs

page 64
Activity 8
1. enero   2. septiembre   3. diciembre   4. diciembre   5. febrero   6. octubre
7. marzo   8. mayo   9. junio   10. noviembre   11. enero   12. octubre

page 70: Mystery Words
junta: from Spanish *junta,* from Latin *jungere* ("to join"). It refers to a group of political plotters or a group seizing power.

gila monster: large, poisonous lizard inhabiting the southwestern United States and northern Mexico

el Niño: a weather condition in which waters in the western Pacific warm up. It causes heavy rains and storms in the western United States as it moves eastward. It is called *El Niño* because it occurs in December and January, during the Christmas season, and refers to the Spanish name for the Christ Child.

Popocatépetl: This is an Aztec word for one of the two volcanoes that overlook Mexico City.

Supplementary Information

I. Linking of the World's Continents

Columbus's voyages explain why Spanish is the language of most of the Americas. His voyages began the link between the Americas and Europe, the Americas and Africa, and the Americas and Asia. The links had both positive and negative effects. A recent exhibit, called *Seeds of Change,* highlighted people, animals, plants, minerals, and diseases that went from the Eastern Hemisphere to the Western and vice versa. For information on it, write to the Smithsonian Institution, Museum of Natural History, Washington, D.C. 20560. For more information, see also *In Search of Columbus*, the January 1992 issue of *National Geographic.*

II. Photographs of Hispanic World

A monthly magazine titled *Geomundo* usually has beautiful photographs of the Hispanic world. For information, write to: Editorial America, SA, Subscription Dept., Box 10950, Des Moines, IA 50347.

Resource Materials

Note: For addresses of publishers and distributors, refer to Appendix A, Master Address List.

Teacher Materials

Books

Spain, Houghton Mifflin, 1993. (Insight Guide series)

Language Materials

How to Pronounce Spanish Correctly, National Textbook. (Useful for help in Spanish pronunciation)

Spanish for Travelers, Berlitz. (Accompanying tape useful for help in pronouncing Spanish)

Ticket to Spain, Passport Books. (Tape useful for pronunciation of basic Spanish phrases)

Pamphlets

Culturgrams on Hispanic countries, Center for International Studies, Brigham Young University

Class Materials

I. Language Materials

Easy Spanish Crossword Puzzles, National Textbook.

Let's Learn Spanish Picture Dictionary, National Textbook.

Spanish in Ten Minutes a Day, Bilingual Books.
Spanish Sign Language, National Textbook.

II. Student Newspapers/Magazines

Americas (English version) (Available by writing to P.O. Box 2103, Knoxville, IA 50197)

Chicos (Children) and *Vamos* (Let's Go). Available from Midwest European Publications, Inc. (Comic book format)

¿Qué Tal? (How Goes It?). Available from Delta Systems.

III. Videos

Ballet Folclórico Nacional de México, Gessler Publishing. (Video with English worksheets)

Cantemos en Español, Picaflor Productions. (Sing-along video)

History of Hispanics in America (Videos), Society for Visual Education, 1985.

Videos available from Knowledge Unlimited:
　　Culture of Spain
　　Mexican People and Culture
　　People of the Caribbean

IV. Posters

Available from Barclay School Supplies: *Portraits of Mexican Americans*

Available from Knowledge Unlimited:
　　Aztec Cosmos Poster
　　Hispanic Heritage Poster series

V. Software

Anagramas Hispanoamericanos, Gessler Publishing. (Hispanic countries and capitals) (For Apple II)

Basic Spanish Vocabulary Builder on Computer, Lingo Fun. (For Apple II)

Spanish Hangman, Lingo Fun. (For Apple II)

VI. Wall Maps/Desk Maps

Available from Rand McNally: Spain, South America, Mexico, and the Caribbean; Map of the Languages of the World

VII. Realia

Available from National Textbook and World Press: badges, buttons, T-shirts

VIII. Cooking Experiences

Vamos a cocinar una comida mexicana. Available from the Kiosk. (Recipes given in English and Spanish, geared to student cooking)

IX. Games/Songs

Land Ho!/¡Tierra Tierra!, World Awareness. (Discovery game in Spanish and English)

Let's Play Games in Spanish, National Textbook.

Songs for the Spanish Class, National Textbook.

X. Multicultural Background Reading

Caribbean, Silver Burdett, 1979.

Christmas in Mexico, National Textbook.

Christmas in Spain, National Textbook.

Famous Mexican Americans, by J. Morey and W. Dunn, Penguin, 1989.
  (Fourteen biographical sketches)

Fiesta! Cinco de Mayo, by June Behrens, Mainline Book Company, 1989.

Hispanic America, Place-in-World Publishers, 1984. (Collection of materials)

Mexican American Folklore, by John O'West, 1989. Available from Social
  Studies School Service.

The Mexicans in America, by June Pinchot, Lerner Publications, 1989.

Puerto Rico: Its History and Culture, by Karl Wagenheim, Continental Press,
  1989.

Spain, Silver Burdett, 1989.

Story of the Moors in Spain, by Stanley Poole-Lane, Baker & Taylor, 1986.

Useful Addresses

Embassy of Spain
Cultural Office
Suite 214
2600 Virginia Avenue, NW
Washington, DC 20037
(For materials on Spain)
Note: For other Spanish-speaking countries, check addresses of their embassies by consulting the telephone directory for Washington, DC, available in public libraries.

Mexican Ministry of Tourism
777 Third Ave.
New York, NY 10017
(For materials on Mexico)

Organization of American States (OAS)
1889 F St., NW
Washington, DC 20006
(For classroom materials, including flag chart)

Puerto Rico Federal Affairs Administration
734 Fifteenth St., NW
Washington, D.C. 20005
(For maps, material on foods; history, legends, art)

CHAPTER 6
EXPLORING FRENCH AND THE FRENCH-SPEAKING WORLD

Goal

To introduce students to the French language and French-speaking peoples; to develop students' awareness of the connections between English and French

Objectives/Outcomes

After working with this chapter, students should be able to:

1. Understand and say a limited number of French expressions and to recognize them in print and be able to write them, including numbers, greetings, classroom directions, restaurant words

2. Name places where French is spoken in the world (including areas of the United States)

3. Demonstrate knowledge of the geographic location of francophone countries

4. Name some famous French scientists, artists, etc., and their contributions; for example, Braille and Pasteur

5. Name at least five words in English that came from French

6. Show their understanding of the role that France played in the history of the United States

7. Point out elements of French culture in the U.S.

Testing for the chapter should be based on these outcomes. (See Assessment in the Methodology section of this manual.)

Implementing the Chapter

Preparation

1. Decorate the classroom with materials relating to France and French culture (e.g., travel posters of France and French-speaking countries in Africa/Caribbean, maps of France and francophone countries). Have a French corner with books about French culture and French-speaking countries, as well as realia (e.g., French coins). Use recordings of French music for atmosphere.

2. *Warm-up.* Ask students to write two words or ideas that come to mind when they hear the word *French*. Use this information as the point of departure to talk about France and French by discussing, confirming, expanding or supporting the student-generated information.

3. Teach students French greetings (found in the text). You might introduce them through a song like "Happy Birthday."

Presentation

Teach the language sections concurrently with sections that deal with geography, culture, and other general topics. (See page 10 in the Methodology section on how to organize a class period.)

Each lesson should include a practice segment in the language explored. Refer to Language Learning Strategies and Activities (see pages 11 to 13) to supplement those in the chapter. (It is recommended that the language segment of the period be conducted in French as far as possible.) Refer to the French Pronunciation Guide, at the end of the text chapter, for help in pronouncing words. You might also want to get some simple language learning tapes to check pronunciation. (See Resource Materials.)

1. For the section about the French in the United States, refer students to French place names in chapter 3. Have them list at least five place names

of French origin. If there are French place names in your part of the country, have students identify them and investigate their meaning.

2. For the *Borrowings from French* section, refer students to chapter 3, on the role French played in the history of English. Have students explain why French had a strong influence on the English language.

3. In the language section, encourage students to actively use the French they are learning. For numbers, have students create their own activity like Activity 6, page 60 in the Spanish chapter in the text. For classroom commands, have them do a "Simon Says" game. Encourage students to act out the dialogues in the text and develop ones on their own (greetings, restaurant).

Additional/Follow-up Activities

1. *Audiovisual activity.* Obtain the filmstrip/cassette *Get in the Swim*, available from the American Association of Teachers of French (see Useful Addresses at the end of this chapter), about why to study French. Have a group (no more than four) prepare to present it to the class, including providing tasks for the viewers to do.

2. *French treasure hunt.* Have students be detectives to find French words in everyday life. They can report on French in the supermarket (say cheese! or *fromage!*), in a clothing store, at the cosmetics counter, in a restaurant. Students could also prepare scrapbooks showing examples of the use of French words and expressions in newspapers, magazines, and advertisements on radio and TV.

3. *Travel agents.* Using the pictures in the text as a springboard, have students role-play being travel agents, telling of some of the tourist sites to visit in France, Canada, the Caribbean Islands, or French-speaking Africa.

4. *Francophone countries.* Have students write to embassies/tourist offices of French-speaking countries to request pamphlets with both historical and current information about the country. Each student should write to a different country.

   Instruct students to use proper standards for correct business writing. After materials are received, a sharing display should be arranged, for example, a bulletin board or an exhibit corner.

5. *French posters.* Have students create posters showing French expressions used in English such as *C'est la vie!, déjà vu, Répondez s'il vous plaît (RSVP)* or French foods such as croissants, éclairs, brie. The posters can be straightforward or humorous.

6. *Flags and mobiles.* Students can make cloth flags of French-speaking countries and incorporate them into mobiles to hang in the classroom.

7. *Days and months.* To supplement the language section of the text, present the days of the week and the months of the year in French.

   Days

lundi [luhn*dee*]	Monday
mardi [mahr*dee*]	Tuesday
mercredi [mayrkre*dee*]	Wednesday
jeudi [zhuh*dee*]	Thursday
vendredi [vahn*druh*dee*]	Friday

samedi [sahm*dee*]	Saturday
dimanche [dee*mahn*sh]	Sunday

Months

janvier [zhahn*vyay]	January
février [fayvree*yay*]	February
mars [mahrs]	March
avril [ahv*reel*]	April
mai [may]	May
juin [zhooehn*]	June
juillet [zhooee*yay*]	July
août [oo]	August
septembre [sehpt*ahm*bre]	September
octobre [ohk*to*br]	October
novembre [nohv*ahm*bre]	November
décembre [day*sahm*bre]	December

* Vowel in the preceding syllable has a nasal sound.

Answer Key

page 76
Activity 1
1. Seine   2. *Countries:* Spain, Belgium, Luxembourg, Germany, Switzerland, Italy; *Bodies of water:* English Channel, Atlantic Ocean, Mediterranean Sea

Activity 2
1. Louis Braille   2. Rodin   3. Victor Hugo   4. radioactivity

page 81
soup du jour: soup "of the day", used to refer to the soup on the menu for the particular day

à la carte: means "from the menu." Ordering à la carte means ordering individual items from a menu, rather than a set menu that is usually offered at a reduced price.

eau de parfum: Eau means "water"; *parfum* is "perfume."

bon voyage: means "good trip" (for leave taking)

page 89
Mystery Words:
Rendezvous: meeting or meeting place
mayday: the international distress signal, used by ships and planes. It represents the sound spelling of the French *m'aider* ("help me").

Supplementary Information

I. Travel

A special ongoing program for travel to Quebec, called *Québec culturel*, is designed for middle school students and their teachers. It is a ten-day trip, with many planned cultural activities in the city of Quebec, including two nights with a host family.

For information, write to:

NASSP School Partnerships
International Office
1904 Association Dr.
Reston, VA 22091

A Primer for Taking Secondary Students to France, by Jim Becker, contains more information about student travel. It is available from:
Modern Language Publications
University of Northern Iowa
Cedar Falls, IA 50613

II. Language Connections

A. Here are some English words that came from names of French people for students to investigate:

chauvinist: means fanatical devotion to one's group or country, from Nicolas Chauvin, a French soldier fanatically devoted to Napoleon

guillotine: refers to a machine of execution in which a person's head is cut off, from Joseph Guillotin (1738-1814), the French doctor who proposed it. It became famous during the French Revolution.

silhouette: an outline of an object, filled in with solid color, from Etienne de Silhouette

B. Additional expressions to use as mystery words: coup d'état, coup de grâce, suite, crêpes

III. French *Sesame Street*

The French Canadian children's program called *Téléfrançais* might be presented. It has been found to appeal to secondary school students of French. Write to:
TV Ontario
Suite 163
4825 LBJ Freeway
Dallas, TX 75244

IV. Reverse Borrowing

Many English words are used in French. Here are a few: *le weekend, le sandwich, le blue-jean, cool et clean, good et fun, c'est too much.*

Resource Materials

Note: For addresses of publishers and distributors, refer to Appendix A, Master Address List.

Teacher Reference

Books

France, Houghton Mifflin, 1993. (Insight Guide series)

France: Its People and Culture, National Textbook. (General background information about the history and culture of France and the contributions of famous French people)

Switzerland: Its People and Culture, National Textbook.

Language Materials

How to Pronounce French Correctly, National Textbook. (Useful for help in French pronunciation)

French for Travelers, Berlitz. (Accompanying tape useful for help in pronouncing French)

Ticket to France, Passport Books. (Tape useful for pronunciation of basic French phrases)

Pamphlets

Culturgrams on French-Speaking Countries, Center for International Studies, Brigham Young University

Class Materials

I. Language Materials

Can You Speak French?, *Mini Page,* March 28, 1988. (Language and cultural activities geared to the middle school)

Easy French Crossword Puzzles, National Textbook.

French in Ten Minutes a Day, Bilingual Books.

French Sign Language, National Textbook.

Let's Learn French Coloring Book, National Textbook.

Let's Learn French Picture Dictionary, National Textbook.

II. Student Newspapers/Magazines

C'est facile! (It's Easy!) Available from Midwest European Publications.

Môme (Child) and *Allons* (Let's Go). Available from Delta Systems.

III. Videos

France, In Love with Paris, World Press. (Video Visits Series)

Glimpses of West Africa (English edition), Gessler Publishing.

Martinique et Guadeloupe, Gessler Publishing. (Filmstrip and video in English)

Visions of Africa, Volumes I and II, Available from Social Studies School Service. (Two videocassettes; includes Senegal, Ivory Coast)

IV. Posters

Available from Gessler Publishing, Teacher's Discovery, and Wellness Reproductions (emotions posters with French expressions)

V. Software

La carte de France (Map of France), Gessler Publishing Company. (For Apple II) (Geography in English)

French Hangman, Lingo Fun. (For Apple II)

VI. Wall Maps/Desk Maps

Available from Rand McNally and Teacher's Discovery

VII. Realia

Available from the Kiosk, National Textbook, Teacher's Discovery, Claudia's Caravan, World Press, and J. Weston Walch, Inc.: Flags, badges, pins, T-shirts

VIII. Cooking Experiences

Cooking the French Way, Lerner Publications, 1982.

A Taste of French Cooking, World Press, 1976.

IX. Games/Songs

Le Loup du nord, by Matt Maxwell. Available from National Textbook. (Audiocassette with songs)

La Marseillaise. Available from Applause Learning Resources. (The music with the history of the song)

Sing-along French Songs and Proverbs. Available from Applause Learning Resources. (Audiocassette)

Sing, Dance, Laugh, and Eat Quiche, French-for-Fun Company. (Audiocassette)

Songs for the French Class, National Textbook.

Additional materials available from Applause Learning Resources, J. Weston Walch Publishing, and Teacher's Discovery.

Vocabulary Games, World Press.

X. Multicultural Background Reading

Africa 1991, Holmes & Meier Publishing, New York, NY, 1991.

Canada, Library of Nations, 1988.

Christmas in France, National Textbook.

The French in America, by Virginia Kunz, Lerner Publications, 1990.

Haiti in Pictures, Lerner Publications, 1987.

Ivory Coast in Pictures, Lerner Publications, 1988.

Mali in Pictures, Lerner Publications, 1990.

Senegal, Mainline Book Company, 1988.

West Indies, Steck-Vaughn, 1991.

Useful Addresses

American Association of Teachers of French (AATF)
57 East Armory Ave.
Champaign, IL 61820
(Some available items: the filmstrip/cassette *Get in the Swim*, on why to study French; a map of Paris showing monuments; postcards; French greeting cards, books about French-speaking areas)

French Cultural Services
972 Fifth Ave.
New York, NY 10021

French Embassy
4101 Reservoir Rd., NW
Washington, DC 20007

French Government Tourist Office
628 Fifth Ave.
New York, NY 10020

Howard University
Foreign Language Department
Washington, DC
(For information on francophone Africa)

Indiana University
Woodburn Hall 221
Bloomington, IN 47405
(For materials, lists on francophone Africa)

Lafayette Convention and Visitors Commission
P.O. Box 52066
Lafayette, LA 70505
(Information on the "capital of French Louisiana")

New Orleans Visitors Center
1520 Sugar Bowl Drive
New Orleans, LA 70112

Quebec Government Office of Tourism
1300 Nineteenth St., NW, Suite 220
Washington, DC 20036

CHAPTER 7
EXPLORING GERMAN AND GERMAN-SPEAKING AREAS

Goal

To introduce students to the German language and culture; to help them understand the recent historical changes in Germany; to increase students' awareness of the relationship of English and German

Objectives/Outcomes

After working with this chapter, students should be able to:

1. Understand, say, read, and write the German material in the chapter, including the numbers from 1 to 30, greetings, names of German foods

2. Name countries where German is spoken

3. Identify recent geographical and historical changes in Germany

4. Name some famous German-speaking people, such as Roentgen and Steinmetz, and their contributions

5. Discuss the history of Germans in the United States and places where they settled

6. List several English words that are borrowed from German

7. Discuss how and why English and German closely resemble each other

8. Identify a number of typical German foods

Testing for the chapter should be based on these outcomes. (See Assessment in the Methodology section of this manual.)

Implementing the Chapter

Preparation

1. Decorate the room with materials relating to German-speaking areas and German culture (e.g., travel posters of Germany and other German-speak-

ing countries such as Austria and Switzerland). Have a German corner with books about German culture. Use recordings of German music for atmosphere. The decor could include pictures of German-style foods, such as *der Frankfurter*.

2. *Warm-up.* Have students look through the chapter and identify words that resemble English words. Explain the importance of German in the history of English (see chapter 3 in the text).

3. Introduce the word *deli*. Ask, "What complete word does it stand for?" Elicit *delicatessen*. Ask, "Did you know it is a German word?" Have students look up the word in a dictionary and explain its origin. Elicit the meaning of the word *essen*, to eat.

4. Teach some basic greetings from the text the first day.

Presentation

Teach the language sections concurrently with sections that deal with geography, culture, and other general topics. (See page 10 in the Methodology section on how to organize a class period.)

Each lesson should include a practice segment in the language explored. Refer to Language Learning Strategies and Activities (see pages 11 to 13) to supplement those in the chapter. Refer to the transcriptions in the text for help in pronouncing words. You might also want to get some simple language learning tapes for pronunciation.

1. As students work in the first part of the chapter, have them point to locations on maps. Have available a map showing the two Germanys before they were reunited.

2. Begin the language study in the chapter with activity 4, reading the German text. As a follow-up, have students make a list of German words in the text that are similar to English words, giving both the German and the English equivalent.

3. Refer students to chapters 3 and 4. Have students explain why German and English are so closely connected.

4. For the study of numbers, have students create their own activity like Activity 6, page 60, in the Spanish chapter in the text, giving answers in German.

5. Encourage students to act out the dialogues in the text and develop ones on their own (greetings, restaurant).

Additional/Follow-up Activities

1. *German discovery.* Have student investigate and locate German names in their surroundings: e.g, German place names, German foods, German businesses. Have students report on their findings, making lists of the German words. As an extension, have students do research on the parts of the United States in which Germans settled (such as Baltimore, Cincinnati, Milwaukee, Philadelphia).

2. *Travel guides.* Have students role-play being travel agents, using pictures (including those in the text). Have them tell of some of the tourist sites to visit in Germany, Austria, and Switzerland.

3. *German history study.* Ask a group of students to prepare a report about the two Germanys and the events that led to reunification. Have them investigate the history of the formerly divided city of Berlin.

4. *German music.* Have interested students investigate music composed by German-speaking composers and report back to class, using tapes if possible. Mozart's *The Magic Flute* and Beethoven's *Fifth Symphony* would be examples of works for them to report on.

Answer Key

page 97
Mozart and Haydn were born in Austria.

page 98
Activity 1
Examples: Mercedes-Benz, BMW, Volkswagen

Activity 2
Baltimore, New York City, Cleveland, Cincinnati, Milwaukee

page 102
22, zwei und zwanzig; 23 drei und zwanzig; 24, vier und zwanzig; 25, fünf und zwanzig; 26, sechs und zwanzig; 27, sieben und zwanzig; 28, acht und zwanzig; 29, neun und zwanzig

page 105
Tagesuppe: soup of the day

page 108
Mystery Words
Glockenspiel: from *die Glocke* ("bell"), *spiel* ("playing a musical instrument"). It refers to a set of bells and mechanical figures often put into clock towers to play when the hour strikes; it also is a musical instrument played by striking hammers on bells or chimes.

Kindergarten: means "garden for children." *Garten* is German for *garden.* *Kinder* means "children."

Blitz: from *Blitzkreig* ("lightning war"). *Blitz* is German for *lightning. Kreig* means "war." It refers to violent, rapid warfare. *Blitz* is now used in English as both a noun and a verb. The noun often refers to a concentrated media campaign aimed at the public in order to sell a product. A media *blitz* uses radio, TV, newspapers, and magazines for that purpose.

Supplementary Information

I. The Amish

The Amish are a German-speaking religious sect that came to the United States in 1728 after fleeing from Bern, Switzerland, and moving from country to country in Europe. William Penn, the Quaker founder of Pennsylvania, offered them asylum. Hence, they are called "Pennsylvania Dutch" (from *Deutsch*). The way of life of the Amish has changed little since they came. They do not accept the innovations of the modern world, such as electricity, cars, telephones, and television. These peace-loving people try to keep their own way of life, avoiding contact with the outside world. Their church services are conducted in German. Amish children go to their own schools, where they are taught English and German. The area of

Lancaster County, Pennsylvania, where many Amish live, is visited by many people each year. They want to observe first hand the way of life of the "Pennsylvania Dutch." Since the early days, Amish have spread to other states, including Iowa, Indiana, and Illinois, and to Canada. Students might be interested in learning more about the Amish. Here are two recommended books: *The Amish*, by Doris Faber, Doubleday, 1991 (with color photographs) and *Meet the Amish*, by Fred Israel, Chelsea House, 1986.

Students should understand that the German spoken by the Amish differs from that of modern Germany because languages keep changing.

II. Germany and Technology

Germany has contributed historically to the development of technology. Have students investigate these Germans:

    Steinmetz—electricity
    Porsche—automobile
    Gauss—magnetism

III. Germany in Europe

Because of its size and leadership in industry, Germany is one of the key countries in the European Community (EC), the economic and political organization of countries in Western Europe. You might have students log current mentions of Germany in the news.

IV. Baron Munchhausen

Baron Munchhausen became famous in the eighteenth century for extraordinary tales of his life as a soldier. His stories were used as the basis for a volume that became widely known and popular in many languages. Students may enjoy reading versions of these tales.

Resource Materials

Note: For addresses of publishers and distributors, refer to Appendix A, Master Address List.

Teacher Reference

Books

Austria: Its People and Culture, National Textbook. (General background information about the history and culture of Austria and contributions of its famous people)

Christmas in Germany, National Textbook.

Germany: Its People and Culture, National Textbook. (General background information about the history and culture of Germany and contributions of its famous people)

The New Germany, Houghton Mifflin, 1993. (Insight Guide series)

Switzerland: Its People and Culture, National Textbook. (General background information about the history and culture of Switzerland)

Language Materials

German for Travelers, Berlitz. (Accompanying tape useful for help in pronouncing German)

How to Pronounce German Correctly, National Textbook. (Useful for help in German pronunciation)

Ticket to Germany, Passport Books. (Tape useful for pronunciation of basic German phrases)

Pamphlets

Culturgrams on various German-speaking countries, Center for International Studies, Brigham Young University.

Class Materials

I. Language Materials

Easy German Crossword Puzzles, National Textbook.

German Sign Language, National Textbook.

Let's Learn German Picture Dictionary, National Textbook.

II. Student Newspapers/Magazines

Das Rad (Bicycle). Available from Delta Systems.

Fertig . . . los (Let's Go) and *Kinder* (Kids). Available from Midwest European Publications, Inc.

III. Videos

Berlin Wall Video, Teacher's Discovery.

Discovering Germany, Available from Applause Learning Resources.

German Folk Dancing Video, Gessler Publishing.

Germany, World Press. (Video Visit Series)

IV. Posters

Wall posters of German foods available from Applause Learning Resources

V. Software

Apfelschuss, Lingo Fun. (Hangman game) (For Apple II)

Basic German Vocabulary Builder, Lingo Fun. (For Apple II)

VI. Wall Maps/Desk Maps

Available from Gessler Publishing Company and Rand McNally

VII. Realia

Available from National Textbook and World Press: Pins, badges, flags

VIII. Cooking Experiences

Cooking the German Way, by Helga Parnell, Lerner Publications, 1988.

IX. Games/Puzzles/Songs

Let's Play Games in German, National Textbook.

Songs for the German Class, National Textbook.

Word Search/Simple Crossword Puzzles, World Press.

X. Multicultural Background Reading

Germany, Silver Burdett, 1991. (People and Places Series)

These Strange German Ways, Gessler Publishing, 1991.

Useful Addresses

German Information Center
950 Third Ave.
New York, NY 10022
(For materials on Germany)

Goethe Institute
Language Department
1014 Fifth Ave.
New York, NY 10028
(For free teaching materials about contemporary Germany)

Langsam Library
University of Cincinnati
Cincinnati, OH 45221
(For materials relevant to German Americans)

CHAPTER 8
EXPLORING ITALIAN, ITALY, AND ITS PEOPLE

Goal

To introduce students to the Italian language by presenting some basic words and phrases; to introduce students to Italy past and present, its many contributions to civilization, especially those in art, music, and science

Objectives/Outcomes

After working with this chapter, students should be able to:

1. Understand, say, read, and write the basic Italian expressions in the chapter, including greetings, names of the days and the months, basic classroom commands and vocabulary, numbers, and foods

2. Describe where Italy is located and name some of its famous cities

3. Describe Italy's two periods of greatness and Italy's contributions to civilization

4. Name and describe the accomplishments of some well-known Italian and Italian American painters, scientists, and musicians such as Da Vinci, Marconi, and Galileo

5. Explain the meaning of common musical terms from Italian

6. Explain the meaning of English words from Italian introduced in the chapter

Testing for the chapter should be based on these outcomes. (See Assessment in the Methodology section of this manual.)

Implementing the Chapter

Preparation

1. Decorate the classroom with materials relating to Italian culture (e.g., travel posters, map of Italy). Have an Italian corner with books about Italy and Italian culture. Use recordings of Italian music for atmosphere.

2. *Warm-up.* Present the material in the *Italian Connection* below. You might want to prepare a transparency with the material or write it on the broad. Elicit responses from individual students or from students organized in teams.

Figure 4

The Italian Connection

What is the Italian connection when we . . .

- Eat pizza, spaghetti, lasagne, gelato? What are some other foods you can add to the list?
- Hear Luciano Pavarotti or Mario Lanza sing? *[famous opera singers]*
- Listen to the radio? *[invented by Marconi]*
- See a picture of the *Mona Lisa*? *[painted by Da Vinci during the Renaissance]*
- See clothes inspired by Italian designers?
- Hear records by singers like Frank Sinatra or Perry Como?
- Hear about public figures past and present, such as Mayor Fiorello La Guardia of New York, Governor Mario Cuomo of New York, Supreme Court Justice Scalia?
- Watch a movie with Al Pacino, Robert De Niro, or Joe Pesci?
- See the Ninja Turtles? *[named after four Italian Renaissance artists]*
- Celebrate Columbus Day? *[discuss the pros and cons of Columbus's voyages]*

As a summary, ask students to tell what they already know about Italy's contributions to the world and contributions of Italian Americans in the U.S. Can they identify any areas in which Italians have made particular contributions?

Presenting the Chapter

Teach the language sections concurrently with sections that deal with geography, culture, and other general topics. (See page 10 in the Methodology section on how to organize a class period.)

Each lesson should include a practice segment in the language explored. Refer to Language Learning Strategies and Activities (see pages 11 to 13) to supplement those in the chapter. Refer to the transcriptions in the text for help in pronouncing words. You might also want to get some simple language learning tapes for pronunciation.

1. Assign individual students a topic on Italian culture as they begin the chapter. Have them present their oral reports as the class works through

the chapter. Suggested topics: Famous Italian and Italian Americans mentioned in the chapter, Italian places (Rome, Florence, Milan, Venice, Naples, Pompei, Vesuvius)

2. For the musical term sections, play famous excerpts from Italian operas, such as the triumphal march from Verdi's *Aida* and Figaro's aria from Rossini's *Barber of Seville*. Try to find selections students may have heard in commercials and have them identify where they have heard them before. Use motivational activities to interest students in this type of music.

   Also, if possible, with the help of the music department, obtain samples of sheet music. Have students list the Italian words telling directions for playing the music.

3. For the Italian food section, obtain a menu from an Italian restaurant. Explain the dishes listed.

4. Encourage students to actively use the Italian language they are learning. For example, have students role-play the Italian greetings presented in the chapter, count objects in Italian, and create simple dialogues.

Additional/Follow-up Activities

1. *Unit project.* Have individual students or groups of students do a unit project on Italy. Some suggestions are to prepare an information booklet on Italy; an Italian travel brochure; posters with Italian places, famous personalities, or Italian products.

2. *Italian foods.* Have students do a project on Italian foods. Have them visit an Italian food store or a supermarket. Have students list all the Italian foods they find and give a brief description of each. Have them check dictionaries and cookbooks to see that the names of all the items are spelled correctly.

3. *Italian Day.* With students, arrange for an Italian day at the school, with the cooperation of the school cafeteria. Have students prepare a written menu of Italian foods. Have groups of students from the class teach schoolmates about the foods and how to say *Buon giorno, Buon appetito,* etc. They may greet the school in Italian over the public address system.

4. *Italian art.* Have interested students do research on Italian artists and their works and present their findings to class. Help them obtain reproductions of famous paintings from the school or public library, or the school art department.

Answer Key

page 112
Activity 1
1. Europa   2. penisola   3. Roma   4. antica   5. antica

page 118
Activity 4
allegro, "happy," quick and lively; andante, slow; crescendo, gradually increasing in force; staccato, "detached," with breaks between notes; piano, softly; forte, loud

page 121
Activity 5
1. camera   2. fresco   3. umbrella   4. maestro, oboe, opera, organ, piano, prima donna, sonata, stanza, trombone, violin   5. fresco, miniature, tempera

page 124
Mystery Words
1. The motto, "Fatti maschii e parole femine," is from the coat of arms of the Calvert family, founders of Maryland. It means "manly deeds and womanly words." It has raised controversy with some women's groups.

2. *Cello* is from *violoncello*, the largest instrument in the violin family.

page 125
Mystery Place
The Leaning Tower of Pisa is in the town of Pisa in the central west part of Italy. The scientist Galileo experimented there and documented the law of falling bodies in physics. The tower continues to lean more and more, and the Italian government is trying to find ways to slow this process and save the tower.

Supplementary Information

I. Pinocchio

Pinocchio is an Italian classic famous worldwide. It was published in 1876 by Carlo Collodi, whose real name was Carlo Lorenzini. The story was the subject of a Walt Disney film. Have interested students report on the book or film.

II. Ninja Turtles

These movie turtles were given the names of famous Italian artists of the Renaissance: Leonardo da Vinci, Michelangelo, Raphael, and Donatello. Have interested students locate at least one work of art by each of these artists and report to the class.

III. Madonna

Madonna is an Italian word that is used to refer to Mary, the mother of Jesus in the Christian religion. Many Italian paintings of the Renaissance have the "Madonna and Child" as their subject. The Christ child is called *Il Bambino*, which means "baby" in Italian. The word *madonna* was also once used to refer to a married woman, equivalent to the modern French *Madame*. (*Donna* in Italian means "woman.") Now *signora* is used to refer to a married woman.

IV. Italian Folk Songs

Italian popular songs are familiar around the world. See the text for "Santa Lucia," a song from Naples in the south of Italy. See the video *The Three Tenors* for a rendition of "O Sole Mio."

Resource Materials

Note: For addresses of publishers and distributors, refer to Appendix A, Master Address List.

Teacher Reference

Books

Christmas in Italy, National Textbook.

Unto the Sons, Gay Talese, Knopf Publishers, 1991. (Saga of Italian American immigrants from early days through the present; the Italian American equivalent of *Roots*)

Language Materials

How to Pronounce Italian Correctly, National Textbook. (Useful for help in Italian pronunciation)

Italian for Travelers, Berlitz. (Accompanying tape useful for help in pronouncing Italian)

Ticket to Italy, Passport Books. (Tape useful for pronunciation of basic Italian phrases)

Pamphlets

Culturgrams on Italy, Center for International Studies, Brigham Young University.

Class Materials

I. Language Materials

Basic Vocabulary Builder, National Textbook.

Easy Italian Crossword Puzzles, National Textbook.

Italian Sign Language, National Textbook.

II. Student Newspapers/Magazines

Azzurro (Blue). Available from Midwest European Publications.

Ciao. Available from Midwest European Publications.

III. Videos/Filmstrips

Rome, World Press. (Video Visits Series)

Available from Applause Learning Resources:

Rome: The Eternal City, Treasures of Italy, Vidal in Venice (videos); *A Day in the Life of an Italian Student* (filmstrip/audiocassette)

IV. Posters

Cartoon posters, Gessler Publishing.

Vocabulary posters, Gessler Publishing Company.

V. Software

Italian Basic Vocabulary Builder on Computer, National Textbook. (For Apple II)

VI. Wall Maps/Desk Maps

Available from National Textbook and Rand McNally

VII. Realia

Available from National Textbook and World Press: Pins, flags, etc.

VIII. Cooking Experiences

Cooking the Italian Way, Lerner Publications, 1986.
Pasta Cookbook, James McNair, Chronicle Books, 1990.

IX. Games/Songs

International Bingo, Gessler Publishing.
Songs for the Italian Class, National Textbook.

X. Multicultural Background Reading

The Italian Americans, by J. Phillip DiFranco, Chelsea House, 1988.
Italy, Silver Burdett, 1986. (People and Places Series)
Italy, by Cinzia Mariella, Franklin Watts, 1986.
Life in an Italian Town, National Textbook.

Useful Addresses

Italian Government Travel Office
630 Fifth Ave.
New York, NY 10011
(For information about Italy, maps, and posters)

The National Italian American Foundation
666 Eleventh St., N.W.
Suite 800
Washington, D.C. 20001
(For information about Italian Americans)

Publishers Choice
Box 4171
Dept. DF10-PD
Huntington Station, NY 11746
(For free information about Italian Americans)

CHAPTER 9
EXPLORING RUSSIAN, RUSSIA, AND ITS PEOPLE

Goal

To introduce students to the Russian language, thereby giving students firsthand experience with a language using a non-Roman alphabet; to introduce students to a few aspects of Russian history and culture

Objectives/Outcomes

After working with this chapter, students should be able to:

1. Recognize and say the basic Russian greetings presented in the chapter

2. Recognize the Cyrillic alphabet, name some of its letters, and discuss how it came to be; give the meaning of *transliteration*

3. Recognize a sample of written Russian

4. Write in Cyrillic cursive from memory the Russian word for "thank you," as practiced in the chapter

5. Count to 10 in Russian and be able to recognize the words for the numbers in Cyrillic

6. Give examples of English words borrowed or derived from Russian

7. Discuss the geography of Russia and its past and recent history in general terms

8. Discuss some aspects of Russian culture and famous Russians, including names of Russian ballets and of Russian composers

Testing for the chapter should be based on these outcomes. (See Assessment in the Methodology section of this manual.)

Implementing the Chapter

Preparation

1. Decorate the classroom with materials relating to Russia (e.g., travel posters, map of Russia). Have a Russian corner with books about Russia and Russian culture and realia (such as nesting dolls).

2. *Warm-up.* Teach students the Russian greeting "pree*vyet*" and have them greet classmates, shaking hands. Present the Cyrillic spelling of the greeting, found in the text. Point out that Cyrillic is a non-Roman alphabet.

3. If available, show the segment of the animated film *Fantasia* that features the "Waltz of the Flowers" from Tchaikovsky's *Nutcracker*.

Presenting the Chapter

Teach the language sections concurrently with sections that deal with geography, culture, and other general topics. (See page 10 in the Methodology section on how to organize a class period.)

Each lesson should include a practice segment in the language explored. Refer to Language Learning Strategies and Activities (see pages 11 to 13) to supplement those in the chapter. Refer to the transcriptions in the text for help in pronouncing words. You might also want to get some simple language learning tapes for pronunciation.

1. Once students have read the section on Russian history, have students bring news items on Russia to class. Create a collage on a bulletin board. Because of the continuing changes in the former Soviet Union since the fall of Communism, it is important for both the teacher and students to keep abreast of current developments.

2. Have students present information on Russian geography (main features), climate, time zones, referring to a wall map. Information can be obtained from encyclopedias or references listed in Resource Materials.

3. Here is a special project for helping students learn the Cyrillic alphabet: Assign each student a letter of the alphabet to illustrate in a novel way (e.g., draw a large letter on tagboard, cut out, and cover with beads, sequins or dry cereal; cut out the letter from wood, with adult assistance). Use the letters in hands-on games.

4. Encourage students to actively use the Russian they are learning: to use Russian greetings and count objects in Russian.

Additional/Follow-up Activities

1. *Unit project.* Have individual students or groups of students do a unit project on Russia. Some suggestions are to prepare an information booklet; a travel brochure; booklets or posters with Russian places, famous personalities, or Russian products.

2. *Interview.* Have a recent immigrant from Russia come to class and have students conduct an interview. Students should prepare a list of questions in advance. Students can ask about political changes, ways of life (buying food, living conditions), and so on.

3. *Review game.* The entire class can devise a game utilizing as much of the information learned in the chapter as they can. Each student contributes a question. A committee can come up with format for playing a game.

4. If a recording of the folk song "Kalinka" is available, a group of students may devise a simple folk dance for the class to learn and perform.

Answer Key

page 129
Activity 1
preevyet, hello; spahseebuh, thank you; dah zveedahnyah, good-bye

page 133
Activity 3
Moscow (capital city); Bolshoi (theater); G.U.M. (shopping); St. Basil (cathedral)

page 135
Language Connections: Refer to the answers for Activity 1
English Words from Russian:

babushka: a head scarf, so named because such scarves are commonly worn by grandmothers (*babushka* means "grandmother" in Russian)

balalaika: Russian musical instrument resembling a guitar, but with a triangular shape

borscht: Russian soup containing meat stock, cabbage, onions, and beet juice (which gives it its red color). Also spelled *borsch*.

Bolshevik: the political party that seized power in the Russian Revolution in 1917 and that later became the Communist party

mammoth: very large extinct kind of elephant (earlier Russian name *mamot*)

sable: small mammal found in northern Europe and Asia, valued for its fur (Slavic name *sobol*)

samovar: a metal urn used for heating water for tea (Russian *sam* means "self" and *varit'* means "to boil"; so the word means "self-boiler")

steppe: level treeless plain

troika: Russian sleigh pulled by three horses; can refer to a group of three rulers *tundra:* vast treeless plain with permanently frozen ground

vodka: Russian alcoholic beverage (In Russian, *vada* means "water." So *vodka* really means "little water.")

page 139
History Connection: Alaska

page 141
For Super Sleuths:
1. *Czar* is used to refer to a person having great power in a certain area, such as drug enforcement. It was the name for the rulers of Russia and comes from the Latin name Caesar, who was a Roman general and dictator.

2. *Caviar* is from Italian *caviari*, which in turn comes from the Turkish *havyar*.

Topics for Discussion and Review
4. kulak, a wealthy peasant; ukase, an edict; Samoyed, a kind of dog used to pull sled; kasha—a mush made from buckwheat

7. cosmos—from Greek for *universe*, nauta—from Latin for *sailor*

8. the purchase of Alaska in 1867

page 142
Mystery Word
Sputnik means "fellow traveler." It was the name given to the first satellite that orbited the earth, launched by the former Soviet Union on October 4, 1957.

Supplementary Information

I. Ballet

Ballet is one of Russia's most prestigious cultural gifts to the world. The Bolshoi theater in Moscow and the Kirov theater in St. Petersburg are famous places where ballets such as Tchaikovsky's *Swan Lake, Sleeping Beauty*, and *Nutcracker* are performed. Female ballet dancers are called *ballerinas* (which is an Italian word meaning "dancers").

II. Grandfather Frost

Grandfather Frost (whose name is pronounced "*dyod* mar*oz*" in Russian) is the Russian Santa Claus. He brings gifts to children on the night of December 31. He can be dressed in red with white trimming, blue with white, or white with white.

Resource Materials

Note: For addresses of publishers and distributors, refer to Appendix A, Master Address List.

Teacher Reference

Books/Articles

"The End of the U.S.S.R.," *Mini Page,* March 1, 1992.

"Moscow: The City around Red Square", *National Geographic,* January 1979, pp. 2-14. (Superior photographs)

The New Russians, by Hendrick Smith, Random House, 1990.
Russia, Houghton Mifflin, 1993. (Insight Guide series)

Language Materials

Russian for Travelers, Berlitz. (Accompanying tape useful for help in pronouncing Russian)

Pamphlets

Culturgram on Russia, Center for International Studies, Brigham Young University.

Magazine **ДАВАЙ!**

(pronounced "da*vah*-ee") (Recommended for teachers who have novice-high or better level of proficiency)

Class Materials

I. Videos/Filmstrips

Moscow and Leningrad (St. Petersburg), World Press.
Available from Applause Learning Resources:
Russian Folk Songs and Dances
A Russian Journey

II. Language Materials

Russian in Ten Minutes a Day, Bilingual Books.
Teach Me Russian. Available from Applause Learning Resources. (Audiocassette) (Use this in the planned lessons on Russian language)

III. Posters

Vocabulary and topical posters available from Gessler Publishing

IV. Software

The Russian Disk, Lingo Fun. (For Apple II, IBM) (Helps teach the Cyrillic alphabet)

V. Maps

Available from Rand McNally

VI. Realia

Available from Kamkin Russian Bookstore (see address below)

VII. Cooking Experiences

Cooking the Russian Way, Lerner Publications, 1986.

VIII. Games/Songs

Peter and the Wolf Ballet, Bellerophon Books. (Coloring book)
Songs for the Russian Class, National Textbook.

IX. Multicultural Background Reading

Empire of the Czars, by Marquis de Custine, Doubleday, 1990.

Journey across Russia, by Bart McDowell, National Geographic, 1977.

Land and People of the Soviet Union, by William Andrews, HarperCollins, 1991. (Still useful despite its out-of-date title)

Russia, Silver Burdett, 1986. (People and Places Series)

Useful Addresses

Kamkin's Russian Book Store
4956 Boiling Brook Parkway
Rockville, MD 20852
(Source for realia, recordings, games, as well as books)

Russian Studies Center
Box 788
Choate-Rosemary Hall
Wallingford, CT 06492
(Provides resource materials for Russian programs in the U.S.)

CHAPTER 10
EXPLORING JAPANESE, JAPAN, AND ITS PEOPLE

Goal

To give students basic information about the Japanese language and present some basic Japanese words and expressions; to give students a glimpse of Japanese history and culture

Objectives/Outcomes

After working with this chapter, students should be able to:

1. Use the Japanese greetings presented in the text

2. Recognize Japanese in print

3. Count to 10 in Japanese

4. Discuss some facts about the Japanese language, as presented in the chapter

5. Explain the ways in which Japanese is written, incorporating some of these terms: *kanji, kana (hiragana, katakana), romaji*

6. Give examples of English words from Japanese

7. Discuss and name some Japanese foods

8. Discuss the geography of Japan and its past and recent history, including its relationship with the United States since World War II

9. Discuss a few aspects of Japanese culture

Testing for the chapter should be based on these outcomes. (See Assessment in the Methodology section of this manual.)

Implementing the Chapter

Preparation

1. Decorate the classroom with materials relating to Japan (e.g., travel posters, map of Japan). Have a Japanese corner with books about Japan and realia (such as origami).

2. *Warm-up.* Ask students to tell what they know about Japan. Write down responses, categorizing them by language, food, geography, history, customs, and so on. Close the activity by summarizing, clarifying, and correcting the information generated.

3. Present a video or a filmstrip on Japan.

4. Introduce the greeting *konnichi wa* the first day. (See text.)

Presentation

Teach the language sections concurrently with sections that deal with geography, culture, and other general topics. (See page 10 in the Methodology section on how to organize a class period.)

Each lesson should include a practice segment in the language explored. Refer to Language Learning Strategies and Activities (see pages 11 to 13) to supplement those in the chapter. Refer to the transcriptions in the text for help in pronouncing words. You might also want to get some simple language learning tapes for pronunciation.

1. Before beginning the chapter, have students discuss the projects listed in "Activities and Projects" at the end of the chapter and choose one as early as possible so that reports on these projects can be scheduled in a staggered fashion.

2. When students have read the section on "Japanese Words You Know," have them guess the meanings of these Japanese words, which are borrowed from English or which English has borrowed: *beisboru* (baseball), *gorfu* (golf); *banzai* (means "ten thousand years" and was used as a Japanese war cry or a cheer); *honcho* (used in U.S. slang to mean the chief or head of a group; from Japanese *han* "squad," *cho* "leader"); *karaoke* (practice in Japanese night clubs and restaurants of patrons singing or performing); *san* (title of respect for both males and females, first or last name, e.g., Sahomi-san, Tanaka-san).

3. Encourage students to actively use the Japanese they are learning, including greetings.

Additional/Follow-up Activities

1. *Geography.* Divide the class into teams of four. Distribute outline maps of Japan with dots indicating major cities. Teams consult a wall map of Japan and fill in names of cities, islands, and geographic features. Have teams report to class, each on a different item (mountains, rivers, islands, cities, seaports) with one team member using a pointer to indicate places.

2. *Art project.* Interested students may produce the *kanji* and *hiragana* characters for *person* (found in the text) out of tagboard, decorate them, and hang them as classroom mobiles.

3. *Holidays.* Have interested students choose a Japanese holiday and report on specific customs for each. There are several holidays especially for

children. If possible, encourage students to make or show something that is related to the holiday. Information on holidays is available in encyclopedias and books on Japan.

4. *Haiku.* Have students write haiku poems and decorate them; place final products on the bulletin board. Haiku is a kind of traditional Japanese poetry, usually describing images of nature, such as the seasons, landscapes, animals, and personal experiences. Here are some characteristics of haiku:

   - Have three lines
   - Do not rhyme
   - Usually have *five* syllables in the first line, *seven* in the second line, and *five* in the third
   - Deal with one topic per poem
   - Use words sparingly, no repetitions
   - Use special words that immediately evoke the image in the reader's mind

   For more information on haiku, refer to *My Own Rhythm: An Approach to Haiku*, by Ann Atwood, Charles Scribner's, 1973.

   Examples:

   > Old pond, blackly still—
   >
   > frog, plunging into water,
   >
   > splinters silent air.
   >
   > (Written three hundred years ago by the haiku poet, Basho)

   > *Butterflies*
   > Butterflies are like
   > a many-colored rainbow.
   > Nectar is their gold.
   > (Written by an American student)

5. *Additional language activity.* Do this activity or ones like it. The task is for students to complete a short paragraph, filling in Japanese words.

   Before you present the activity, introduce the following Japanese words that are not in the text:

   - hai, pronounced "hi," means yes
   - ohayo gozaimasu, pronounced "ohio gazaeemahs," means good morning (used before 10 A.M.)
   - kombanwa, pronounced "kom bahn wa," good evening

   Japanese Words to Use: hai, sayonara, konnichiwa, ohayo gozaimasu, kombanwa, arigato, Osaka

   Reading

   My name is Yoshie, and I come from the second-largest city in Japan, called ______. I will teach you the words to say in Japanese for greetings. In the morning before 10 A.M., say ______, after 10 A.M and in the afternoon, say ______, and in the evening, say ______. If you would like to visit me in Japan one day, say ______. Whenever I give you a gift from Japan, tell me ______. I must go now and you should say to me ______.

Answer Key

page 147
Activity 1
1. tea   2. Tokyo   3. group   4. four   5. Pacific/west   6. Hawaii

page 149
Activity 2
B. 1. No (The spoken languages belong to different families.)   2. 3 (kanji, kana, romaji)   C. 1. kanji   2. hiragana

page 151
Activity 3

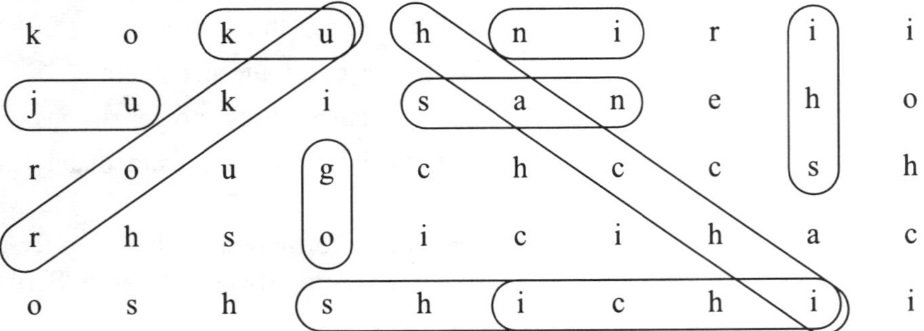

page 152
Activity 4
1. bata—butter   2. supu—soup   3. choppu—chop   4. hamu—ham
5. beikon—bacon   6. sosu—sauce   7. sarada—salad   8. chizu—cheese
9. remon—lemon   10. dezato—dessert   11. naifu—knife   12. kohi—coffee

Supplementary Information

I. Japanese Sports

Japanese young people are very fond of sports. The most popular are baseball, swimming, skiing, soccer, volleyball, ice skating, and roller skating. *Sumo* (wrestling) is known as the national spectator sport of Japan. Most of the wrestlers begin training in their early teens. They eat and drink large quantities in order to reach weights of 265 pounds or more. The best-known martial arts are iaido, budo, judo, kendo, karate.

II. China's Influence on Japan

Historically Japan borrowed and modified important ideas and inventions from the Chinese (including characters for writing). In ancient times and during the Middle Ages, Chinese was considered the language of scholarship in the Orient. Japanese scholars studied in China. From the Chinese, the Japanese learned about architecture, the use of metal, the silk industry, improvement of textiles, building of bridges, among other things. Buddhism, which originated in India, spread to Japan from China in the sixth century A.D.

III. Teens in Japan

School attendance in Japan is 240 days a year, including Saturdays, compared to 180 days in the United States. The school year begins on April 1 and ends March 31 the following year. Japanese students spend a lot of time studying. In addition to regular school, many attend private schools called *jukus*, in order to prepare for exams, such as those that determine whether they go on to college. Write to Marjis (see Useful Addresses) for detailed information about the Japanese school day and school policies.

IV. Origami

The art of paper folding began in China, but the Japanese gave it the name *origami*, from *ori* (folding) and *kami* (paper). The *k* of *kami* is pronounced like a *g* in this case. Origami is one of the traditional arts of Japan. For more information, refer to *The Complete Book of Origami*, by Robert J. Lang, Dover Publications.

V. More Food Facts

- Bean curd is made from soybeans.
- *Natto* is fermented soybeans.
- *Soba* is buckwheat noodle. (The correct way to eat *soba* is to "slurp"—no chewing.)
- *Cha-bola* is buckwheat noodles made with green tea.
- Pumpkin and cucumber blossoms and chestnut leaves are also eaten.
- One unusual custom is the giving of chocolate kisses in fancy wrapping on Valentine's Day. Note: They are given by women to men.

Resource Materials

Note: For addresses of publishers and distributors, refer to Appendix A, Master Address List.

Teacher Reference

Books

Contemporary Japan, 1988. Available from Social Studies School Service.

Everything Japanese, National Textbook, 1992.

Japan, An Illustrated Encyclopedia, Kodansha, 1993.

Japan in the Classroom, by Jacquelyn Johnson, Social Science Education Consortium, 1993.

Japan Today!, National Textbook, 1986.

The Japanese Today, by Edward Reischauer, Harvard University Press, 1988.

Language Materials

Everyday Japanese, by Edward Schwarz and Reiko Ezawa, National Textbook, 1985.

Japanese in Ten Minutes a Day, Bilingual Books.

Japanese for Travelers, Berlitz. (Accompanying tape useful for help in pronouncing Japanese)

Pamphlets

Culturgram on Japan, Center for International Studies, Brigham Young University.

Class Materials

I. Language Materials

Japanese for Children, National Textbook. (Text with cassette, suitable through middle school)

Fun with Japanese, D'Amours Publishing Company. (See address below) (Language practice set to music, three tapes; set called "Rapanese")

Teach Me Japanese. Available from Apple Learning Resources. (Book and audiocassette)

Teach Me Tapes, Inc. (See address below.)

II. Magazine

Nihongo Journal, Charles E. Tuttle.

III. Videos/Filmstrips

Japan, World Press. (Video Visits Series)

Japan: Asia's Superpower, Knowledge Unlimited. (Two filmstrips/cassettes)

Video Letter from Japan, Asia Society. (See address below.)

IV. Posters

Available from Japan Airlines. (See address below.)

Wellness Poster (Japanese), Wellness Reproductions.

V. Wall Maps/Desk Maps

Available from Rand McNally

VI. Realia

Available from Claudia's Caravan, Gessler Publishing, and National Textbook

VII. Cooking Experiences

Cooking the Japanese Way, by Reiko Weston, Lerner Publications, 1983.

VIII. Games/Songs

Japanese through Games and Songs, Bess Press. (With audiocassette)

Let's Play Games in Japanese, National Textbook, 1992.

IX. Multicultural Background Reading

Children Are Children Are Children, by Ann Cole et al., Little, Brown, 1978. (Section on Japan)

Count Your Way through Japan, by Jim Haskin, Lerner Publications.

Japan: The Land, Japan: The People, Japan: The Culture, Crabtree Publishers, 1991. (Three texts)

The Japanese in America, by Noel Leathers, Lerner Publications, 1991.

Useful Addresses

Asia Society
725 Park Ave.
New York, NY 10021

D'Amours Publishing
26088 Kay Ave.
Hayward, CA 94545

JACP
414 East Third Ave.
San Mateo, CA 94401
(Asian American catalog has authentic materials from Japan and books on Japan.)

Japan Airlines
1666 K St., NW
Washington, DC 20006
(For posters)

Japan America Society of Washington
606 Eighteenth St., NW
Washington, DC 20006

Japan Information and Culture Center
Embassy of Japan
917 Nineteenth St., NW
Washington, DC 20008

Japan National Tourist Organization
630 Fifth Ave.
New York, NY 10011

Kinokuniya Bookstore
10 West Forty-Ninth St.
New York, NY 10020
and
1581 Webster St.
San Francisco, CA 94115

Marjis
Mid-Atlantic Region
Department of Educational Policy
College of Education
University of Maryland
College Park, MD 20742
(Free materials about Japan: customs, schools, young people's activities)

Sakura Bookstore
15809 Frederick Rd.
Rockville, MD 20855

Teach Me Tapes, Inc.
10500 Bren Road East
Minneapolis, MN 55343

CHAPTER 11
EXPLORING CHINESE, CHINA, AND ITS PEOPLE

Goal

To give students basic, though limited, information about the Chinese language and present a few Chinese words and expressions, thus introducing students to a nonalphabetic language; to help students become acquainted with Chinese history and culture

Objectives/Outcomes

After working with this chapter, students should be able to:

1. Understand, say, and recognize in print the Chinese words and expressions in the chapter

2. Recognize the Chinese language in print

3. Write from memory at least two of the Chinese characters practiced in the chapter

4. Discuss some of the main features of Chinese language

5. Explain *romanization* and *pinyin*

6. Name some of the principal geographical features of China, including the countries that border it, its important cities and rivers

7. Respond to questions about Chinese history based on the information in the chapter

8. Describe one or two Chinese holidays or celebrations, such as Chinese New Year

9. Give at least two English words derived from Chinese

Testing for the chapter should be based on these outcomes. (See Assessment in the Methodology section of this manual.)

Implementing the Chapter

Preparation

1. Decorate the classroom with materials relating to China (e.g., travel posters, map of China). Have a Chinese corner with books about China and Chinese culture and realia (such as authentic crafts, Chinese menus).

2. *Warm-up.* Elicit from students the image they have of China and what they know about it. Close the activity by summarizing, clarifying, and correcting the information generated.

3. Show parts of a video on China, or on a Chinese-speaking city like Hong Kong or Taipei.

4. Have students practice the greeting "nee how." Explain the importance of using the correct *tone,* since a change in tone may signify a change in meaning. (See the text for information on tone.)

Presentation

Teach the language sections concurrently with sections that deal with geography, culture, and other general topics. (See page 10 in the Methodology section on how to organize a class period.)

Each lesson should include a practice segment in the language explored. Refer to Language Learning Strategies and Activities (see pages 11 to 13) to supplement those in the chapter. Refer to the transcriptions in the text for help in pronouncing words. You might also want to get some simple language learning tapes for pronunciation.

1. Assign the Activities and Projects in the text to different groups. On "reporting day," each group explains its work to the others.

2. For the *Welcome to China* section, have students go to the wall map and point out various aspects of the geography of China. Have students refer to encyclopedias or other reference materials on China to prepare for the task.

3. Discuss with students foods served at a local Chinese restaurant. Bring in a menu if possible.

Additional/Follow-up Activities

1. *Chinese characters.* Have students make models of Chinese characters practiced in the chapter. These may be hung as mobiles. If calligraphy materials are available, have students practice writing the characters.

2. *Chinese New Year.* The American cities with the most elaborate Chinese New Year's celebrations are San Francisco, New York, and Seattle. Have students write to the Chambers of Commerce of these cities for details of the celebrations. Also encourage them to do research using books. Have students report to the class and, if possible, produce something that relates to the celebration. If the class is studying the chapter during early February, students could simulate New Year's festivities or attend them in a local Chinese American community.

3. *Chinese lunar calendar.* Present the following information on the Chinese lunar calendar (see Figure 5, p. 80):

   The calendar is based on the cycles of the moon (*lunar* means relating to the moon, from Latin *luna*). Each year of the calendar is named after an animal. Another name for the calendar is the Chinese zodiac. It goes from the year of the rat, through twelve years to the year of the pig. Then it begins over again with the year of the rat. The year of a person's birth determines his or her animal sign. The system is not based on science, but it can be fun to discover your animal sign.

   Make sure that in your school and community, the following activity would not be objectionable before you present it: Have students find out their animal year, based on their birth date. Have students compare the Chinese zodiac to the ancient Roman zodiac signs, such as Pisces, Aquarius, Leo, and so on. Have them investigate what the Roman signs were based on (the constellations).

Figure 5

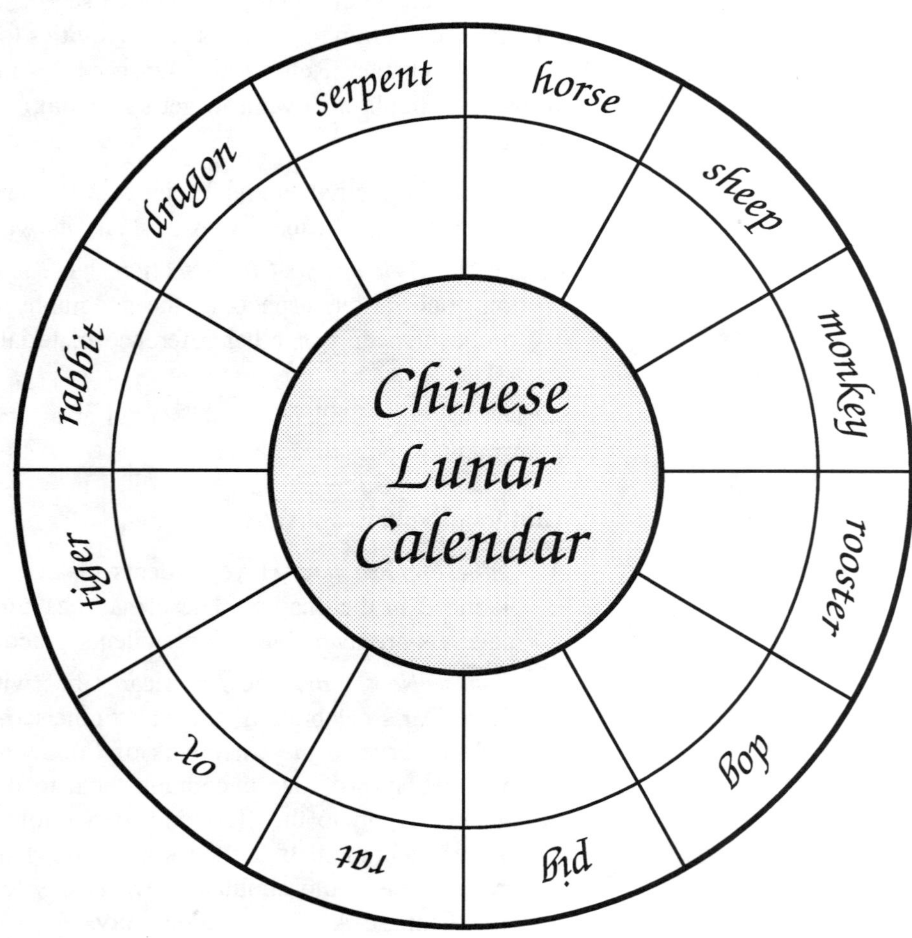

4. *Culminating activity.* Have students plan and prepare presentations for an assembly on Chinese culture, followed by a class field trip to a Chinese restaurant.

Answer Key

page 160
Activity 1

A. The world's largest countries in area are Russia, Canada, Brazil, United States, China.

B. 1. China's neighbors: Pakistan, India, Nepal, Bhutan, Burma, Laos, Vietnam, Taiwan, North Korea, South Korea, Kazakhstan, Russia
2. Ch'ang Chiang (Yangtze) River

page 161
Activity 2

A. Qin dynasty (or Ch'in), 221 B.C. to 207 B.C.; Song dynasty (or Sung), 960 A.D. to 1279 A.D.; Ming dynasty, 1368 A.D. to 1644 A.D.

B. Marco Polo traveled from Italy to China. He brought the following back to Italy: silks, spices, jewels, the idea of paper money, and pasta (although the latter is a matter of controversy).

page 165
Roman alphabet (writing the sounds in)

page 169
Mystery Words: Pekingese, a small toy-type dog originating in China; Chow-Chow, a dog that originated in China or a relish of chopped vegetables sometimes pickled in mustard (pidgin English from Chinese)

Supplementary Information

I. Chinatowns, U.S.A

The following American cities have large Asian American populations: San Francisco, New York, Seattle, Chicago, Boston, Houston, and Washington, D.C. Chinatown in San Francisco has 30,000 inhabitants, occupies 24 city blocks, and has 150 restaurants. It contains the first Chinese Historical Society established in North America, which houses the largest collection of Chinese American artifacts. Chinatown in New York is home to about 150,000 Asians. It includes a Chinese museum and numerous restaurants featuring the cuisines of Asia.

II. Pasta

The theory that Marco Polo brought the idea for pasta back to Italy from China has been challenged. Some people think that pasta originated with the Etruscans, an ancient people of Italy. For more information, see *Pasta*, by James McNair, Chronicle Books, 1990.

III. China

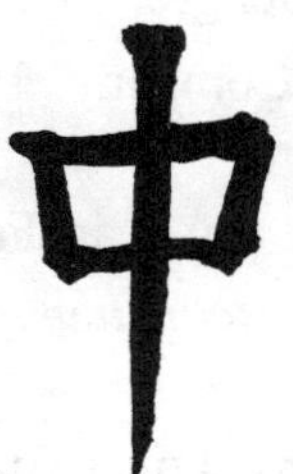

The above character represents the word *China*. Here is an explanation for its shape: the ancient Chinese thought that the earth was square and flat and that China was its center. The Chinese language has been spoken since about 2,000 B.C.

Resource Materials

Note: For addresses of publishers and distributors, refer to Appendix A, Master Address List.

Teacher Reference

Books

China, Houghton Mifflin, 1993. (Insight Guide series)

Language Materials

Chinese for Travelers, Berlitz. (Accompanying tape useful for help in pronouncing Chinese)

Pamphlets

Culturgrams on China and Singapore, Center for International Studies, Brigham Young University.

Class Materials

I. Language Materials

You Can Write Chinese, by Kurt Wiese, Viking Press, 1964. (For students interested in trying their hand at Chinese characters)

II. Videos/Filmstrips

Cities of the Orient: Hong Kong, Singapore, World Press.
Understanding Chinese America, JACP. (See address below.) (Filmstrips/videos)

III. Posters

Available from Applause Learning Resources are posters on various topics such as sports, clothing, school.

IV. Wall Maps/Desk Maps

Available from Rand McNally

V. Realia

Available from JACP (see address below), including abacus, kites, mah jong set

VI. Cooking Experiences

Chinese Food and Drink, Bookwright Press, 1987.

VII. Multicultural Background Reading

China, Globe Book Company, 1987. (Information on history, culture, geography)
China's Long March, by Jean Fritz, G. P. Putnam's, 1988.
Chinese: Recent American Immigrants, by Jodine Mayberry, Franklin Watts, 1990.
Chinese New Year, by Tricia Brown, Henry Holt, 1987.
Lion Dancer, by Hay and Slovenz-Low, Scholastic, 1991.
Strangers from a Different Shore: A History of Asian Americans, by Roland Takaki, Penguin, 1989.

Useful Addresses

Chinese Historical Society of America
17 Adler Place
San Francisco, CA 94133

JACP, Inc.
414 East Third Ave.
San Mateo, CA 94401
(For authentic materials, books, and information on China)

CHAPTER 12
EXPLORING ARABIC AND THE ARABIC-SPEAKING WORLD

Goal

To introduce students to Arabic, a language with a non-Roman alphabet; to help students gain familiarity with Arabic-speaking countries, with the geography of regions where Arabic is spoken, and with Islamic culture; to make students aware of the some of the historical contributions of the Arab world

Objectives/Outcomes

After working with this chapter, students should be able to:

1. Understand, say, and recognize in print the Arabic expressions in the chapter, which include greetings and the numbers from 0 to 10

2. Recognize the Arabic alphabet

3. Discuss basic facts about the Arabic language, as presented in the chapter

4. Name at least ten of the countries where Arabic is spoken

5. Demonstrate knowledge of the geography of the Middle East and North Africa

6. Demonstrate elementary knowledge of the cultures of the Arab/Islamic countries

7. Explain why the numbers we use are called Arabic numbers

8. Name at least three English words from Arabic and give their meanings

Testing for the chapter should be based on these outcomes. (See Assessment in the Methodology section of this manual.)

Implementing the Chapter

Preparation

1. Decorate the classroom with materials relating to the Arab world (e.g., travel posters, maps of the Middle East and North Africa). Have a corner with books about the Arab world and culture, as well as realia, and folk literature such as "Arabian Nights."

2. *Warm-up.* Encourage students to share what they know about the Arabic language and where it is spoken and about the history and cultures of the Arab world. Students should become aware that Arabic is spoken over

several broad regions, and not just one country. Point out that Arabic uses an alphabet, but not the Roman alphabet.

3. Play a video about the Arab world (such as the one on Egypt listed in the Resource Materials for this chapter).

4. Have students practice the Arabic greeting pronounced "as-salaam alaykom" the first day.

Presentation

Teach the language sections concurrently with sections that deal with geography, culture, and other general topics. (See page 10 in the Methodology section on how to organize a class period.)

Each lesson should include a practice segment in the language explored. Refer to Language Learning Strategies and Activities (see pages 11 to 13) to supplement those in the chapter. Refer to the transcriptions in the text for help in pronouncing words. You might also want to get some simple language learning tapes for pronunciation.

1. Have students practice the "welcome" in Arabic expression at the beginning of the chapter.

2. As students do activity 1, part A, have them identify the locations on the wall map. Activity 1, part B, (country information) can be the basis of oral reports throughout study of the chapter.

3. Encourage students to actively use the Arabic they are learning: to use Arabic greetings and to count objects in Arabic.

4. If there is a Middle East restaurant in your area, obtain a menu to use in connection with the study of the food of Arabic-speaking areas.

Additional/Follow-up Activities

1. *"Name That Country" game.* Assign an Arabic-speaking country to each student "secretly." Students research the country and compose a set of clues about the country to present to the class. The class tries to guess the country. The class votes on the most clever set of clues.

2. *Creating word games.* Divide the class into groups. Challenge each group to devise a crossword puzzle or a word search using English words derived from Arabic. Have the groups try to solve one another's puzzles.

3. *Report on the Islamic religion.* Encourage interested students to prepare an oral or written report on the Islamic religion, including, for example, an explanation of the period of *Ramadan*.

4. *Arabian Nights.* Have student volunteers read stories from the *Arabian Nights* to class or act out one of the stories. As a follow-up, invite students to write a story in the style of the *Arabian Nights*. Students could work in groups and produce a story to be published.

5. *English from Arabic.* Present some more English words from Arabic and have students investigate their origins: *chemistry, coffee, magazine*. Have students add to the list of these words.

Answer Key

page 173
Activity 1
A. Algeria, Bahrain, Djibouti, Egypt, Iraq, Jordan, Kuwait, Lebanon, Libya, Mauritania (official language is French, but language of the people is Arabic), Morocco, Oman, Qatar, Saudi Arabia, Somalia, Sudan, Syria, Tunisia, United Arab Emirates, Yemen Arab Republic

Arabic is also spoken in Israel, where it is an official language along with Hebrew.

page 176
Footnote: The word *calligraphy* comes from Greek. In Greek, *kalli* means "beautiful" and the Greek suffix *-graph* means "writing." Suffixes like *-graph* are covered in chapter 16, which is about ancient Greek.

page 177
Footnote: The word *crux* in Latin means "cross." The expeditions to the Holy Land were called Crusades, from this word. The Holy Land has many important Christian religious sites, including the place where Christ died on a cross. The word *crux* in English refers to the essential point, as in the "crux of the matter."

page 178
Notes: The Hebrew word is *shalom.*

page 182
Activity 4
1. b   2. f   3. g   4. h   5. e   6. c   7. d   8. a

page 183
Bonus Word: A mecca is a place to which people come from everywhere, usually people with the same goal or in the same field.

page 184
Mystery Words
mogul: An Indian Muslim descended from one of several conquering groups of Mongols, Turks, or Persians. In English, it now refers to a person of power in a specific area or field.

nadir: the lowest point, from Arabic *nazir*; its opposite is *zenith,* the highest point.

alfafa: a kind of plant often grown for animal feed (from a Spanish word taken from the Arabic)

minaret: the tall slender tower attached to a mosque (from Arabic *manarah,* "lighthouse")

Supplementary Information

I. Arab Cultural Influences

The early Arab and Islamic civilization helped to preserve the writings and ideas of the ancient Greeks and Romans. Between 700 and 1500 A.D., Baghdad (in modern Iraq) was a great center of learning, as was Cordoba in Spain, which the Moors had conquered. These centers influenced thought in Western Europe and were important in the transition of Western Europe from the Middle Ages to the Renaissance.

In Middle Eastern countries, geometric designs are traditionally used to decorate buildings and gardens. Such patterns have influenced artistic design in the West.

II. Facts about Saudi Arabia

The United States has a close relationship with Saudi Arabia. Saudi Arabia is the largest exporter of oil in the world, and thousands of Americans work in the oil fields there.

A large part of the country is desert. Its two important cities are Riyadh, the capital, and Mecca, the holy city of Islam.

Prince Sultan is a famous astronaut from Saudi Arabia.

Clothing: Boys and girls often wear Western-style clothing. Boys and men sometimes wear loose robes and a cloth head covering held in place with a headband. It is traditional for girls after the age of twelve and for women to wear long black robes and to cover their faces with a veil. However, it is true that in cities many people wear modern clothes while others wear traditional clothing.

Sports: Soccer is the national sport. Also popular are camel and horse racing (the Arabian horse is world famous). Often-played games are chess and backgammon.

Shopping: Marketplaces are called *souks.* There are also shopping malls.

III. Language Connections

Note the word *camel* in a number of languages:

kamelos (Greek)

camelus (Latin)

gamal (Hebrew)

chamel (old French) (chameau, "shah-moh" in modern French)

jamal (Arabic)

camel (English)

Resource Materials

Note: For addresses of publishers and distributors, refer to Appendix A, Master Address List.

Teacher Reference

Books

Egypt, Houghton Mifflin, 1993. (Insight Guide series)

History of the Arab Peoples, by Albert Hourani, Harvard University Press, 1991.

Lands, Peoples, and Communities of the Middle East, by Juanita Will Soghikian. (Includes enrichment activities on blackline masters; originally developed at the Center for Middle Eastern studies, Harvard University) (Currently available from Claudia's Caravan or by writing to Juanita Swedenburg, 16105 East Carmel Drive, Fountain Hills, AZ 85268)

Language Materials

Arabic for Travelers, Berlitz. (Accompanying tape useful for help in pronouncing Arabic)

Just Listen 'n Learn Arabic, National Textbook. (Also has travel and cultural information)

Pamphlets

Culturgrams for Middle Eastern countries, Center for International Studies, Brigham Young University.

Class Materials

I. Videos/Filmstrips

The Changing Arab World, Knowledge Unlimited. (Filmstrip/video)

Egypt, World Press. (Video Visits Series)

II. Posters

Arabic alphabet and counting poster available from International Book Centre

III. Wall Maps

Available from Rand McNally and International Book Centre

IV. Realia

Available from the Harvard University Center for Middle Eastern Studies (see address below) and the International Book Centre

V. Cooking Experiences

Cooking the Lebanese Way, Lerner Publications, 1986.

VI. Activities

Arab World Notebook. Available from International Book Centre. (Reproducible sheets covering food, people, culture, history)

VII. Multicultural Background Reading

An Arab Family, Lerner Publications, 1985.
Count Your Way through the Arab World, Carol Rhoda Books, 1991.
A Family in Egypt, Lerner Publications, 1985.
Iraq in Pictures, Lerner Publications, 1990. (Visual Geography Series)
The Lebanese in America, by Elsa Harck Marston, Lerner Publications, 1987.
Lebanon in Pictures, Lerner Publications, 1989. (Visual Geography Series)
Syria in Pictures, Lerner Publications, 1990. (Visual Geography Series)

Useful Addresses

American Association of Teachers of Arabic
Johns Hopkins University
School of Advanced International Studies
1740 Massachusetts Ave., NW
Washington, DC 20036

Harvard University Center for Middle Eastern Studies
Attn: Librarian
Cambridge, MA 02138
(Source of authentic materials and information)

Middle East Studies Association
Department of Oriental Studies
University of Arizona
Tucson, AZ 85721
(For materials on the Middle East)

CHAPTER 13
EXPLORING THE HEBREW LANGUAGE, ISRAEL, AND ITS PEOPLE

Goal

To provide students with a brief experience with the Hebrew language, introducing some of its basic features such as its alphabet and explaining its relationship to other languages; to help students gain familiarity with the history and life of modern Israel

Objectives/Outcomes

After working with this chapter, students should be able to:

1. Understand, say, and recognize in print the basic Hebrew expressions presented in the chapter, including greetings and the numbers to 10

2. Recognize the Hebrew language when encountered in script

3. Give at least three examples of English words derived from Hebrew

4. Demonstrate knowledge of the geography of Israel

5. Discuss the significance of Israel as related to the development of world religions

6. Describe some aspects of life in Israel as presented in the chapter, such as holidays

7. Name at least five Jewish Americans and their accomplishments

Testing for the chapter should be based on these outcomes. (See Assessment in the Methodology section of this manual.)

Implementing the Chapter

Preparation

1. Decorate the classroom with materials relating to Israel (e.g., travel posters, maps, photographs). Have a Hebrew corner with books about Hebrew, the Israeli nation and culture, and appropriate realia.

2. *Warm-up.* Use video, slides, or filmstrips showing contemporary life in Israel.

3. Teach students the greeting "shalom." Have students refer to the Hebrew word in the text the first day.

Presentation

Teach the language sections concurrently with sections that deal with geography, culture, and other general topics. (See page 10 in the Methodology section on how to organize a class period.)

Each lesson should include a practice segment in the language explored. Refer to Language Learning Strategies and Activities (see pages 11 to 13) to supplement those in the chapter. Refer to the transcriptions in the text for help in pronouncing words. You might also want to get some simple language learning tapes for pronunciation.

1. Have students make large versions of Hebrew alphabet letters and use them in games/activities.

2. Encourage students to actively use the Hebrew they are learning: to use Hebrew greetings and count objects in Hebrew. Have students practice the dialogue in the chapter daily.

3. If possible, consult a music teacher for assistance in singing the song in the chapter. It may be sung with students in a circle, greeting one another.

4. Israel is often in the news because of the unsettled political conditions in the Middle East. As students read the information about Israel, have them bring current newspaper articles to class for discussion.

Additional/Follow-up Activities

1. *Food.* Have students investigate Jewish foods: many communities have a Jewish delicatessen; interested students could visit and report back to class. Have students find out about the meaning of the term *kosher* in reference to foods.

2. *Travelog.* Have students work in groups to produce a narrated travelog about Israel to present to class. If possible, help them obtain pictures to illustrate their travel information.

3. *Kibbutz.* Have students look up *kibbutz* in an encyclopedia or other source and write a half page to one page to continue the information in the text. They may check the library for books on Israel. See the list in "Multicultural Background Reading" at the end of this section.

4. *Jewish contributions.* Have students work in groups to make a poster or a bulletin board of contributions of Jewish Americans; it could include names of famous songs written by Jewish composers, Jewish comedians, and so on.

Answer Key

page 192

Activity 3

Bonus Question: Saudi Arabia does not border on Israel.

Activity 4

A. Beersheba, capital city of the Negev, a desert region in southern Israel; Haifa, a busy port in northwestern Israel; Jerusalem, capital of Israel, regarded as a holy city by Jews, Muslims, and Christians; Tel Aviv, largest city in Israel, seaport on the Mediterranean

B. *Albert Einstein:* 1879-1955, world's most famous scientist (in physics), worked on the atomic bomb. He formulated the theory of relativity and the famous equation $E = MC^2$ (energy equals mass times the square of the speed of light). He came to the U.S. from Germany as a refugee from the Nazis during the 1930s.

   Golda Meir: political leader; prime minister of Israel from 1969 to 1974

   Irving Berlin: composer of many popular songs including "White Christmas" and "God Bless America." An immigrant from Russia, he was originally named Israel Baline.

Henry Kissinger: authority on international affairs, secretary of state under President Nixon in the 1970s. He came to the U.S. as a refugee from the Nazis.

George Gershwin: composer of classical and popular music including "Rhapsody in Blue" and the musical "Porgy and Bess"

Barbra Streisand: popular singer

page 195

Mystery Words:

1. Yiddish: See Supplementary Information below.

2. Chutzpah: a Yiddish word meaning "gumption, boldness"

3. *Sábado* is related to the Hebrew word *Shabbat*. The English equivalent is Sabbath.

Supplementary Information

I. Yiddish

Yiddish is distinct from Hebrew. Yiddish is derived from High German dialects, with the addition of some Hebrew words and ones from Slavic languages. It developed in Jewish communities in Eastern Europe. Yiddish is written in the Hebrew alphabet. It is used all over the world in Jewish communities.

Language Connection: The term *Yiddish* is from *jüdisch* (German for "Jewish") and *Diutsch* (an older spelling of *Deutsch,* meaning German). Here are a few examples of Yiddish words:

Mensch, meaning "strong man" in Yiddish (like *macho*). *Mensch* is the German word for *man.*

Oy gevalt, an expression of disbelief ("Oh, my word!")

Hutzpah (see Mystery Word activity answers above)

For more information, refer to *Hurray for Yiddish*, by Leo Rosten, Simon & Schuster, 1982.

II. Television in Israel

There is only one TV channel in Israel. Children watch a program like *Sesame Street*, called "Rkhov Sum Sum" in Hebrew. There are news reports in Hebrew and Arabic. American television programs are shown, with Hebrew and Arabic subtitles.

Note: A program for teaching the Hebrew alphabet and songs modeled after *Sesame Street* is shown on public television in the United States. Videos of the program and a teacher's guide are available from:

Shalom Sesame
P.O. Box 2284
South Burlington, VT 05407

III. The Hebrew Calendar

The Jewish year begins in October. In the Hebrew calendar, 1994-1995 is the year 5754; 1995-1996 is 5755, etc.

IV. Some Food Information

matzo—brittle unleavened bread (made without yeast), eaten especially during Passover

   pita—flat, round bread, originally from other Middle Eastern countries but used extensively in Israel

V. Dreidel

A dreidel (*dra*-del) is a special toy top. It has four sides with Hebrew symbols. It goes back to ancient times when Jewish people were not permitted to worship in their own way. If an enemy approached while they were having services, they would immediately begin spinning the dreidel to distract the intruder. Spinning the dreidel as a game is a Hanukkah custom for Jewish children nowadays.

Resource Materials

Note: For addresses of publishers and distributors, refer to Appendix A, Master Address List.

Teacher Reference

Books

Israel, Houghton Mifflin, 1993. (Insight Guide series)

Language Materials

Hebrew for Travelers, Berlitz. (Accompanying tape useful for help in pronouncing Hebrew)

Pamphlets

Culturgram on Israel, Center for International Studies, Brigham Young University.

Class Materials

I. Magazine

Shofar (in English) (Available from 43 N. Cote Drive, Melville, NY 11747)

II. Videos

Israel, World Press. (Video Visits Series)
Israel: Yesterday and Today, Knowledge Unlimited.

III. Posters

Available from Gessler Publishing
Emotions poster (Hebrew) available from Wellness Reproductions, Inc.

IV. Wall Maps

Available from Rand McNally

V. Realia/Games

Dreidel game. Available from Claudia's Caravan. (See Supplementary Information)
Games and realia are also available from KTAV (see address below)

VI. Cooking Experiences
Cooking the Israeli Way, Lerner Publications, 1986.

VII. Multicultural Background Reading
First Thousand Words in Hebrew, (Usborne) EDC Publishing, 1984.
Israel, Children's Press, 1986.
Israel: A Sacred Land, by Emily Faitz and Sondra Henry, Dillon Press, 1987.
Jewish Family Celebrations, by Arlene Cardozo, St. Martin's Press, 1982.
Passport to Israel, Franklin Watts, 1987.

Useful Addresses

Israel Educational Materials
Israel Center
111 W. Fortieth St.
New York, NY 10018

Israeli Accents
4838 Boiling Brook Pkwy.
Rockville, MD 20902
(Videos, games, realia, books from Israel)

Jewish Publications Society of America (JPSA)
1528 Walnut St., Suite 800
Philadelphia, PA 19102

KTAV
120 East Broadway
New York, NY 10002
(Realia, games)

CHAPTER 14
EXPLORING SWAHILI AND SWAHILI-SPEAKING AREAS

Goal

To introduce students to the Swahili language and areas where it is spoken; to help students become familiar with Africa's contributions to humanity and, through extension activities, the contributions of African Americans; to increase students' awareness of the wealth of Africa's (and the world's) languages

Objectives/Outcomes

After working with this chapter, students should be able to:

1. Understand, speak, read, and write the Swahili expressions presented in the chapter, including basic greetings, numbers, and the words *uhuru* (freedom), *harambe* (together)

2. Count to 10 in Swahili and write the number words from memory

3. Discuss the areas of Central and East Africa where Swahili is spoken; name the countries, their capitals, and scenic places

4. Discuss Africa's gifts to the world

5. Name at least five world-famous people in African history

6. Explain the significance of the African American holiday *Kwanzaa* and how it is celebrated

7. Name at least three African languages in addition to Swahili and tell where they are spoken

Supplemental Outcome

Name at least ten well-known African Americans and their contributions

Testing for the chapter should be based on these outcomes. (See Assessment in the Methodology section of this manual.)

Implementing the Chapter

Note: The main focus of the chapter is on East and Central Africa, where Swahili is spoken. Other regions of Africa are mentioned in specific contexts, such as in "World-Famous People in African History."

Preparation

1. Decorate the classroom with materials relating to areas where Swahili is spoken (e.g., map of Africa, travel posters, photographs) and a Swahili corner with books on Swahili and Swahili-speaking areas of Africa.

2. *Warm-up.* Show a video on Africa to help students acquire an overall perspective.

3. Teach greetings in Swahili the first day: *jambo* or *hujambo* and the response *sijambo* as presented in the chapter. Also teach *kwa heri* (pronounced "kwah *hai*ree"), which means "good-bye."

Presentation

Teach the language sections concurrently with sections that deal with geography, culture, and other general topics. (See page 10 in the Methodology section on how to organize a class period.)

Each lesson should include a practice segment in the language explored. Refer to Language Learning Strategies and Activities (see pages 11 to 13) to supplement those in the chapter. Refer to the transcriptions in the text for help in pronouncing words. You might also want to get some simple language learning tapes for pronunciation.

1. Discuss the geography of East and Central Africa, using the material in the chapter as a starting point. Have students work in groups and fill in outline maps of Africa to show countries and cities where Swahili is spoken.

2. After several days of study in the chapter and language practice, divide the class into teams. Have the teams develop quizzes or games incorporating Swahili expressions and other information in the chapter, such as Swahili facts and African gifts.

3. Have students teach the Swahili dialogue in the chapter to family members.

4. Encourage students to actively use the Swahili they are learning: to exchange Swahili greetings and count objects in Swahili. Have students practice the dialogue in the chapter daily.

5. Have a "geography" bee in which teams identify African countries on an outline map, languages spoken, and major cities.

Additional/Follow-up Activities

1. *Reports.* A student or a group chooses a Swahili-speaking country to investigate and produces a written report that includes a map, information on places and customs of the country, and other interesting facts discovered.

2. *Kwanzaa.* If the chapter is being studied during December, have the class plan a Kwanzaa festival, with the cooperation of the school cafeteria and the principal's office. (Since schools are closed at the end of December, the holiday may be celebrated the previous week.) Refer to the Supplementary Information and Resource Materials sections for this chapter for more information about Kwanzaa useful for the project. The class should also write reports explaining the background of the holiday and the festivities surrounding it and explain what they have learned to other classes.

3. *Swahili exhibit.* Have students collect African artifacts, photographs, and posters and prepare a showcase exhibit. Invite other classes to visit. Students might write to embassies of Swahili-speaking countries for information. Stress proper letter-writing skills.

4. *African Americans.* Have students publish a book on famous African Americans. See Supplementary Information in this chapter for a list of some prominent African Americans.

5. *Wildlife preservation.* In descriptions of East and Central Africa, the native animals, some of which are endangered species, cannot be ignored. Have students write to the following places for more information, using proper standards for business letters:

> World Wildlife Fund
> 1250 Twentieth-Fourth St., NW
> Washington, DC 20037

> African Wildlife Foundation
> 1717 Massachusetts Ave., NW
> Washington, DC 20036

> National Zoo
> 3000 Connecticut Ave.
> Washington, DC 20008

Answer Key

page 199
Activity 1
B. The fact that European languages are spoken in African countries has been the result of the European colonization of Africa. Below is a list of countries that have French, English, or Portuguese as one of their official languages.

French	**English**	**Portuguese**
Benin	Botswana	Angola
Burkina-Faso	Ethiopia	Mozambique
(formerly Upper Volta)	Ghana	Guinea-Bissau
Burundi	Kenya	
Cameroon	Lesotho	
Central African Republic	Liberia	
Chad	Malawi	
Congo	Mauritius	
Côte d'Ivoire (Ivory Coast)	Namibia	
Gabon	Nigeria	
Guinea	Sierra Leone	
Madagascar	South Africa	
Mali	Swaziland	
Mauritania	Zambia	
Niger	Zimbabwe	
Rwanda		
Senegal		
Togo		
Zaire		

page 204

Activity 4

B. 1. Desmond Tutu   2. Jomo Kenyatta (original name: Kaman Johnstone)   3. Haile Selassie   4. Nelson Mandela   5. Christiaan Barnard   6. Julius Nyerere   7. Kwame Nkrumah   8. Léopold Senghor   9. Kipchoge Keino   10. Miriam Makeba   11. Ladysmith Black Mambazo   12. Patrice Lumumba   13. Albert Schweitzer

C. Addis Ababa—Ethopia, Cape Town—South Africa, Dar es Salaam—Tanzania, Dakar—Senegal, Johannesburg—South Africa, Kinshasa—Zaire, Nairobi—Kenya, Pretoria—South Africa. An Arabic name: Dar es Salaam; a Swahili name: Nairobi

page 207

Activity 5

Afrikaans—South Africa; Akan—Ghana; Hausa—Niger, Cameroon; Igbo—Nigeria; Kikongo—Kenya; Kiluba—Zaire; Lingala—Zaire; Shona—Zimbabwe; Xhosa—South Africa; Yoruba—Nigeria, Benin; Zulu—South Africa, Lesotho

Other examples of African languages: Amharic—Ethopia; Bemba—Zambia; Edo—Nigeria; Fulakunda—Guinea-Bissau; Luganda—Uganda; Ijaw—Nigeria; Kanuri—Chad, Cameroon; Rundi—Burundi; Sotho—Lesotho; Temne—Sierra Leone; Tiv—Nigeria, Cameroon; Wolof—Senegal; Zandu—Zaire

Note: World almanacs, published annually, usually have information on the languages of countries around the world.

Supplementary Information

I. Kwanzaa

Kwanzaa is a celebration of African American cultural, social, spiritual, and family values. It was created in 1966 by Maulana Ron Karenga, professor of African American studies at California State University (Long Beach). It is celebrated during the week between Christmas and New Year's. Each day of the celebration has a theme. Included below are the Swahili words for the themes.

12/26	First day: Umoja (Unity)
12/27	Second day: Kujichagulia (Self)
12/28	Third day: Ujima (Work and Responsibility)
12/29	Fourth day: Ujamaa (Cooperative Economics)
12/30	Fifth day: Nia (Purpose)
12/31	Sixth day: Kuumba (Creativity)
1/1	Seventh day: Imani (Faith)

During this time, families get together and perform skits and share potluck meals. The climax of the week is a rich family feast. The colors of Kwanzaa are red, black, and green. Additional information on Kwanzaa, including a calendar and a kit, is available from this address:

Anacostia Museum
(A branch of the Smithsonian Institution)
1901 Fort Place, SE
Washington, DC

II. Legendary Mount Kilimanjaro

Africa's highest mountain is located in Tanzania with a height of 19,340 feet (5,895 meters). It has been part of African legends from ancient times. The local Chagga people referred to the mountain with the phrase *kilemieiroya* ("The mountain cannot be conquered"). To the traders from the coast, who spoke Swahili, this sounded like *kilimanjaro*, hence the name by which we know the mountain.

The peak of Mount Kilimanjaro is always covered with ice and snow, although the mountain is only three degrees below the equator. Many people come from all over the world to climb the mountain. To preserve the wildlife and the environment around the mountain, the Tanzanian government established the Kilimanjaro Forest Reserve and a national park. (Information courtesy of the Embassy of Tanzania, Washington, DC)

III. African Americans in the Old West

Some African Americans became cowboys after the Civil War. Interested students may investigate this topic by writing to *Mini Page,* for the February 16, 1992 issue (see Master List of Addresses).

IV. World-Famous African Americans

This is a reference list of African Americans for class projects. It is not exhaustive, and students may want to include others.

Hank Aaron: baseball player; holds the record for most home runs

Mohammed Ali: boxer of international fame

Arthur Ashe: famous tennis player

Crispus Attucks: during the American Revolution, led a protest group in Boston that culminated in the Boston Massacre (in which American colonists were killed by the British)

James Baldwin: novelist

Benjamin Banneker: inventor, astronomer; helped to plan the city of Washington, DC

Mary McLeod Bethune: adviser to presidents Roosevelt and Truman; founder of a college

Thomas Bradley: well-known former mayor of Los Angeles, California

Gwendolyn Brooks: poet, novelist; winner of a Pulitzer Prize

Ralph Bunche: diplomat, representative to the UN; winner of the Nobel Peace Prize in 1950

George Washington Carver: scientist; worked in plant research

Shirley Chisolm: first African American woman to be elected to the House of Representatives (1968)

Bill Cosby: comedian, entertainer

Benjamin O. Davis, Jr.: first African American Air Force general (His father was the first African American Army general.)

Frederick Douglass: editor, orator, leader of African American causes in the nineteenth century

Dr. Richard Drew: pioneer in developing blood bank

William E. B. Du Bois: founder of the NAACP, 1909

Paul Lawrence Dunbar: poet, novelist

Duke Ellington: musician and composer

James Farmer: a founder of the Congress of Racial Equality

Ella Fitzgerald: legendary popular singer

Florence Griffith-Joyner: runner; winner of three gold medals and one silver at the 1988 Olympics

Alex Haley: author; wrote *Roots*; winner of the Pulitzer Prize

Matthew Henson: member of Peary's expedition to the North Pole, 1909

Benjamin Hooks: executive director of the NAACP until 1991

Lena Horne: famous popular singer and actress

Langston Hughes: poet; story writer

Jesse Jackson: civil rights leader; presidential candidate; "shadow" senator for Washington, DC

Barbara Jordan: distinguished lawyer; former member of Congress

Jackie Joyner-Kersee: winner of three gold medals and one bronze in 1988 and 1992 Olympics. Considered greatest woman athlete in U.S.

Coretta Scott King: civil rights leader; wife of Martin Luther King, Jr.

Martin Luther King, Jr.: slain civil rights leader; winner of Nobel Peace Prize in 1963

Sugar Ray Leonard: boxer; winner of a gold medal at the 1976 Olympics

Donald McHenry: U.S. ambassador to the UN

Malcolm X: Muslim leader; instilled black pride

Thurgood Marshall: first African American justice on the Supreme Court (1967-1991); won pivotal 1954 decision on desegregation

Toni Morrison: novelist; winner of a Pulitzer Prize and winner of the 1993 Nobel Prize for Literature

Carol Moseley-Braun: First African American woman elected to the U.S. Senate (1992)

Jesse Owens: runner; winner of four gold medals at the 1936 Olympics

Rosa Parks: symbol of civil rights movement; citizen of Montgomery, Alabama, who refused to sit at the back of the bus

Colin Powell: first African American Chairman of the Joint Chiefs of Staff (from Jamaica)

Leontyne Price: internationally acclaimed opera singer

Paul Robeson: concert singer

Jackie Robinson: first African American in major league baseball, in 1947

Carl T. Rowan: journalist and author

Debi Thomas: figure skater; winner of a bronze medal at the 1988 Olympics

Sojourner Truth (Isabella Baumfree): educator and abolitionist

Harriet Tubman: an organizer of the underground railroad, smuggling slaves out of the South; also Union nurse and spy during the Civil War

Cicely Tyson: well-known actress

Alice Walker: novelist; author of *The Color Purple*

Booker T. Washington: scientist; founder of Tuskegee Institute

Dr. Daniel Hale Williams: performed one of the first open heart operations (1893)

Richard Wright: novelist

Andrew Young: civil rights leader; president of the National Urban League; U.S. ambassador to the UN

Resource Materials

Note: For addresses of publishers and distributors, refer to Appendix A, Master Address List.

Teacher Reference

Books

Kenya, Houghton Mifflin, 1993. (Insight Guide series)

Zaire, Houghton Mifflin, 1993. (Insight Guide series)

Language Materials

Swahili, Teach Yourself Books, by D. V. Perrott, Random House, 1987.

Swahili for Travelers, Berlitz. (Accompanying tape useful for help in pronouncing Swahili)

Pamphlets

Culturgrams on Swahili-Speaking Countries, Center for International Studies, Brigham Young University.

Class Materials

I. Videos/Filmstrips

Kwanzaa. Available from Claudia's Caravan. (Filmstrip/cassette)

Visions of Africa, Vol. I, Central and East Africa. Available from Social Studies School Service. (Video)

II. Wall Maps/Desk Maps

Available from Rand McNally and Social Studies School Service

III. Realia

Various items available from Claudia's Caravan: flags of African people, "All One People" buttons in Swahili, inflatable animal globe

IV. Songs/Music

Africa Moves, Rounder Records. (Cassette with music from various parts of Africa)

Jambo and Other Call Response Songs and Chants, Rounder Records. (Kenya and Tanzania; includes "Counting in Swahili"; with teacher notes)

V. Activity Materials

Africa Mural Packet, Touch and See Publishing. (With reproducible pages)

Jambo, Hola, Hello, Cultural Connections. (Activity kit with tapes)

Kwanzaa, Children's Press.

Kwanzaa Coloring Book, Claudia's Caravan.

Lessons on Africa, Part IV (Zaire, Kenya, Tanzania, Zimbabwe). Available from Social Studies School Service. (Reproducible pages)

My Ancestors Are from . . . Africa, Touch and See Publishing. (Activity cards)

VI. Multicultural Background Reading

Africa 1993, Holmes & Meier Publishing Company.

African Myths and Legends, retold by Kathleen Arnott, Oxford University Press, 1990.

African Wildlife, by Warren Halliburton, Macmillan Child Group, 1992. (Photographic account)

Aida, Harcourt Brace Jovanovich, 1990. (Leontyne Price retelling the story of the Verdi opera of the Ethiopian princess taken as a slave, with colorful, glossy illustrations)

Globe African American Biographies, Globe Book Company, 1991.

Golden Names for an African People, by Nia Damali, Blackwood Press, 1986. (African and Arabic names and their meanings)

Great African Thinkers, Vol. I, by Ivan Van Setima and Larry Williams, Transaction Books, 1986.

Jambo Means Hello, by Muriel Feelings, Dial Press, 1974. (A Swahili alphabet book)

Kenya, Families around the World Series, 1984. Available from Claudia's Caravan.

Kenya in Pictures, Lerner Publications, 1988.

Tanzania in Pictures, Lerner Publications, 1988.

Zimbabwe in Pictures, Lerner Publications, 1988.

Useful Addresses

African Studies and Research Program
Howard University
Washington, DC 20059

African Studies Center
University of California
Los Angeles, CA 90024

African Studies Program
Northwestern University
630 Dartmouth
Evanston, IL 60201

Reid-C American African Mail Order Book Service
P.O. Box 512
Temple Hills, MD 20757

National Museum of African Art
Smithsonian Institution
950 Independence Ave, SW
Washington, DC 20560

CHAPTER 15
EXPLORING LATIN, ANCIENT ROME, AND ITS PEOPLE

Goal

To introduce the concept of an ancient language that is no longer spoken; to help students become aware of the impact of Latin on the English language and its relationship to the Romance languages; to give an overview of ancient Roman civilization and its influence on the modern world

Objectives/Outcomes

After working with this chapter, students should be able to:

1. Discuss some basic facts about the Latin language and its history
2. Locate Rome on a map and outline the extent of the Roman empire in a general manner
3. Give the meaning of at least five Latin terms or abbreviations that are part of everyday life, such as *E pluribus unum, a.m., p.m., etc., video, e.g.*
4. List at least ten English words with Latin roots and explain the role of the root in the meaning, e.g., *aqualung*
5. Recite or role-play the Latin dialogues in the chapter, employing correct pronunciation
6. Count to 10 in Latin and give at least one English derivative for each number, e.g., *unus-unify*
7. Discuss the role of Latin in medicine, law, science
8. Explain the meaning of the following Latin-based prefixes: *ab-, circum-, con-, inter-, non-, post-, sub-, super-, trans-*

Testing for the chapter should be based on these outcomes. (See Assessment in the Methodology section of this manual.)

Implementing the Chapter

Preparation

1. Decorate the classroom with materials relating to ancient Rome (e.g., maps of the Roman empire, posters showing Roman gods). Obtain charts featuring English derivatives from Latin, Latin abbreviations, and scientific words from Latin, which are available from the American Classical League (see Useful Addresses at the end of this chapter).

2. If Latin charts like those described above in point 1 are available, have students point to words or terms that they understand. Each student should copy a word, prefix, or abbreviation to look up. If charts are not available, provide lists of Latin derivatives from newspapers, magazines, or textbooks for this activity.

3. *Warm-up.* Show a video or filmstrip on ancient Rome (see Resource Materials). Present activities related to the video.

4. To give a general orientation, use copies of *Welcome to Ancient Rome* (see Resource Materials) or the humorous booklet "You Can't Escape Latin," from the American Classical League.

Presentation

1. Assign groups of students various sections of the text. They are to prepare a quiz for their section. Groups exchange quizzes so that all eventually have read each section.

2. Using the Latin words in the chapter as a starting point, have students prepare personal dictionaries of Latin in the world around them. Encourage them to use reference books such as dictionaries and encyclopedias to check the meaning of words.

3. As an aid in presenting the song "Mica, Mica, Parva Stella" (the Latin version of "Twinkle, Twinkle, Little Star"), here is a more direct translation of the Latin:

   Twinkle, Twinkle, Little Star,
   You are truly quite beautiful
   Shining above the world
   Like a jewel in the sky.

Additional/Follow-up Activities

1. *Derivative trees.* Assign a group of students a Latin root for which to find English derivatives. They can draw trees, with the root as the "tree trunk" and derivatives as the "branches."

   Examples:

   Videre: to see
   video, vision, television, revise, supervise, visionary, visible

   Spectare: to look at
   spectator, retrospect, respect, inspect, introspective

   Ducere: to lead
   duct, conduct, produce, reduce, induce

2. *Roman gods.* Have interested students research the Roman gods. Encourage them to retell to the class famous myths, such as that of Tantalus.

3. *Botany.* Have interested students prepare a scrapbook of commonly known flowers and other plants with their Latin scientific names. They can report on why scientific names of plants and animals are in Latin (originated by Swedish botanist, Carolus Linnaeus).

4. *Class assembly.* Have students present a Latin assembly as a culminating activity. It could include a choral recitation of the Latin translation of Martin Luther King's "I Have a Dream Speech" (found in Supplementary Information below). You might have students alternate reciting Latin and English lines in chorus.

5. *Roman banquet.* Arrange a Roman banquet with students dressed in ancient Roman costume. For information, see the references under "Cooking Experiences" in Resource Materials.

6. *Latin word detectives.* Challenge students to find the Latin origin of the following terms:

   Canary Islands: so named by the ancient Roman author Pliny the Elder because there were said to be an unusual number of dogs on the islands (*canaria* means "pertaining to a dog" in Latin and has nothing to do with canaries)

   spectrum: refers to a band of colors formed when white light breaks up (like a rainbow effect); from Latin *spectare*, "to look at"

   ultra: means "beyond"; *ultraviolet* means beyond the violet part of the spectrum (compare with *ultrasound* and *ultramodern*)

   infra: means "below"; *infrared* means below the red part of the spectrum (compare with *infrasonic, infrastructure*)

   antebellum: means before the war; used to refer to the period in U.S. history before the Civil War

   quincentennial: 500th anniversary, e.g., Columbus's voyages

7. *Roman tour.* Have students act as tour guides for a visit to the sites of ancient Rome, such as the Forum and the Colosseum.

Answer Key

page 213
Activity 2
century, cent ("one hundred"), one hundred years; unit, un(i) (unus—"one"), a single item; terrestrial, terr (terra—"land"), pertaining to the earth; oculist, ocu (oculus—"eye"), eye expert

page 216
Activity 4
grateful—gratias (thanks), satisfied—satis (sufficient), agitate—agis (you are doing, moving)

page 217
Activity 5
unified, unus; duet, duo; September, septem; octagon, octo; decimals, decem
page 219
Activity 6
A. XIX, 19; XXX, 30; XCI, 91; MDCCLXXVI, 1776
page 220
Activity 7
1. March   2. August   3. January   4. July   5. April   6. May   7. June
8. September, October, November, December

Activity 8
 A. Mercury, Venus, Earth, Mars, Jupiter, Saturn, Uranus, Neptune, Pluto

 B. terra, earth; sol, sun; luna, moon; mare, sea
page 222
Activity 9
B. alma mater, "nurturing mother," the school you graduate from; in memoriam, in memory of; post mortem, after death; terra firma, solid ground; versus, against
page 223
Abbreviation Review
 1. for example, e.g., exempli gratia

 2. that is, i.e., id est

 3. in the year of the Lord, A.D., Anno Domini

 4. and others, et al., et alii

 5. before noon, a.m., ante meridiem

 6. after noon, p.m., post meridiem

 7. postscript, P.S., post scriptum

 8. pound, lb., libra

 9. and so forth, etc., et cetera
page 224
Big Dipper and Little Dipper, Polaris
page 226
Mystery Words
 1. *Extraterrestrial:* from *extra,* "outside of" and *terra,* "earth"; refers to things coming from beyond the planet Earth

 2. *K-9 Corps:* refers to police dogs, from "K-9," the pronunciation of *canine,* from the Latin word for *dog*

 3. *muscle:* from Latin *mus,* for "mouse"

 4. *SPQR:* stands for *Senatus Populusque Romanus,* "The Senate and the Roman People." This was the motto of ancient Rome. It is still seen on public works in modern Rome.

Supplementary Information

Latin in Today's World

Radio Finland and Radio Austria broadcast a five-minute weekly news bulletin in Latin, which can be received on shortwave. The producers of the broadcasts must constantly coin new Latin expressions.

Example: Communitas rerum publicarum independentium
Commonwealth of Independent States

For information about the Finnish broadcasts, write to Nutii Latini, Kristina Kanolin/JA 58, Finnish Broadcasting Company, Box 10, 00241 Helsinki, Finland, (3580) 14801. In addition, the Vatican in Rome regularly broadcasts cultural programs in Latin.

Resource Materials

Note: For addresses of publishers and distributors, refer to Appendix A, Master Address List.

Teacher Reference

Books

English from the Roots Up, 1990. Available from the American Classical League. (Background information on English derivatives from Latin)

Latin for Even More Occasions, by Henry Beard, Villard, 1992. (Latin equivalents for humorous English expressions)

Latin in American Schools, by Sally Davis, Scholars Press, 1991.

Rome, 2,000 Years Ago. (Published in Italy and available from the American Classical League)

Women in Ancient Greece and Rome, by Michael Massey, Cambridge University Press, 1988.

World Mythology, by Donna Rosenberg, National Textbook, 1986.

Language Materials

Classical Dictionary, National Textbook.

Magazines/Journals

Pompeiiana Newsletter. (See address below.) (Interesting material about ancient Roman culture.)

Prima. Journal of Elementary Teachers of Classics. Available from American Classical League. (Includes information about Latin in schools, activities, stories of ancient times, in English)

Class Materials

I. Student Magazine

Adulescens (Young Person, Youth). Available from Midwest European Publications.

Calliope, Cobblestone Publishing. (Articles and projects about Roman and Greek history, archaeology, games, word origins)

II. Videos/Filmstrips

The Greeks and the Romans, Knowledge Unlimited. (Filmstrip/cassette, with
    teacher guide)

Mythology Is Alive and Well, Guidance Associates. (Video)

Rome, World Press. (Video Visits Series)

Victims of Vesuvius, Guidance Associates. (Video)

III. Posters

Available from the American Classical League: Preamble to the U.S. Constitution
(showing words derived from Latin), vocabulary charts, derivatives charts, mythology posters, *cave canem* (beware of dog) poster, Colosseum
    Available from World Press: Latin parchment posters and vocabulary posters
(animals, parts of the body)

IV. Software

Latin Hangman, Lingo Fun. (For Apple II)

Available from the American Classical League:

Escape from Pompeii (For Apple II) (Adventure simulation)

Hypermyth (Macintosh) (Animated text of stories of classical mythology)

V. Wall Maps/Desk Maps

Available from Rand McNally (Roman empire)

VI. Realia

Available from World Press: badges, thank-you (*multas gratias*) cards

Available from Bolchazy-Carducci Publishing: badges with Latin sayings, such
    as *carpe diem* ("seize the day")

VII. Cooking Experiences

Ancient Rome, by Simon James, Random House, 1990. (Contains section on
    Roman foods)

The Romans, by Pamela Odijk, Macmillan, 1989. (Contains section on Roman
    cooking)

VIII. Songs

Available from the American Classical League:

Latin Songs and Carols (Latin versions of familiar songs)

Mythology Songbook (Musical versions of familiar myths using well-known
    tunes)

Sing Along in Latin

IX. Activities

Ancient Rome, by Susan Purdy and Cass Sandak (Civilization Project Book),
    Franklin Watts, 1982. (Hands-on projects)

The Romans Pop-up, by Andy and Maggie Hall, 1992. Available from the
    American Classical League.

Themes for Classical Studies, by Ashley Carter et al., Cambridge University
    Press, 1991. (Reproducible maps, worksheets about ancient Greece and
    Rome)

X. Multicultural Background Reading

Graeco-Roman Sports and Games, by Rudolph Masciantonio, American Classical League.

Mythology and You, by Donna Rosenberg and Sorelle Baker, National Textbook, 1992.

The Roman Origins of Our Calendar, American Classical League. (Also includes festivals and holidays of ancient Rome)

The Romans, by A. J. Marks and G. I. F. Tingay, Usborne. Available from the American Classical League.

Romans and Their Empire, by Graham Tingay and John Badcock, Dufour Editions, 1992.

Welcome to Ancient Rome, by Anne Millard, National Textbook, 1987.

Ye Gods!, by Helen Britt, Longman, 1987. (About Greek and Roman mythology)

Useful Addresses

American Classical League
Miami University
Oxford, OH 45056
(Main source of teaching materials for Latin)

Pompeiiana Newsletter
6026 Indianola Ave.
Indianapolis, IN 46220

CHAPTER 16
EXPLORING ANCIENT GREEK AND THE ANCIENT GREEK WORLD

Goal

To briefly present *classical* Greek and its contributions to the English language; to help students become aware of ancient Greece as one of the early civilizations that greatly influenced the Western world

Objectives/Outcomes

After working with this chapter, students should be able to:

1. Discuss some basic facts about ancient Greek

2. Recognize and be able to recite letters of the classical Greek alphabet; name at least two uses of it in modern times

3. Give ten Greek roots or prefixes used in English, with their meanings

4. Locate Greece on a map and name at least one of its famous landmarks

5. Discuss at a basic level some of the contributions of the ancient Greeks to modern thinking (philosophy) and mathematics and science

6. Explain the origin of the Olympic games

Supplemental Outcome

Identify the most famous figures of Greek mythology; explain mythology

Testing for the chapter should be based on these outcomes. (See Assessment in the Methodology section of this manual.)

Implementing the Chapter

Note: Modern Greek expressions are given in the Supplementary Information section. You may want to teach these as part of the chapter.

Preparation

1. Decorate the classroom with materials relating to ancient Greece (e.g., map of ancient Greece, posters showing Greek gods). Greek prefixes and roots in large letters may be placed around the room. A time line should also be on the wall to help students understand the concepts of B.C. and A.D. Charts and posters are available from the American Classical League (see Useful Addresses at the end of this chapter).

2. *Warm-up.* Have a brainstorming session with the class about what they know about ancient Greece and Greek. The Greek prefixes and roots displayed (see point 1 above) could be incorporated into the discussion.

3. Present a list of famous ancient Greeks or Greek gods and goddesses. Have students choose one to investigate and describe or role-play the person for the next class. Possible names: Socrates, Plato, Archimedes, Pythagoras, Euclid, Demosthenes, Zeus, Hermes, Poseidon, Athena, Hera.

4. Teach the modern Greek greeting "yi*asso*" (hello) and the classical Greek (*hi*ray) (found in the text). Point out that ancient Greek is not the same as modern Greek, illustrating the concept of language change.

Presentation

1. Have students make large versions of Greek alphabet letters and use them in games/activities or for mobiles.

2. As students read the first section, have each produce a personal fact sheet on the ancient Greek language.

Additional/Follow-up Activities

1. Have the class create a bulletin board display with Greek derivatives or expressions whose meaning is derived from Greek history or with well-known mythological images

    Examples: Achilles' heel; titanic effort; Atlas holding the earth; Apollo (god of the sun) driving a chariot across the sky; symbol of the medical world (the original Greek symbol consisted of one snake, a symbol of healing, around the staff of Aesculapius [Asklepios], a legendary physician; the modern medical symbol has two snakes in some versions and only one in others)

2. Plan an all-class presentation for a school assembly about the original Olympic games and their modern version. Students should describe and illustrate the most important athletic events. The February 2, 1992 issue of Mini Page is entirely devoted to this topic (see Master List of Addresses).

3. Have a student team investigate and report on Priestley's discovery of oxygen, chlorophyll, and the process of photosynthesis. Use the presentation to point out the environmental concept of the importance of green plants. Emphasize that the scientific words *oxygen, chlorophyll,* and *photosynthesis* are derived from Greek and have students investigate their meanings (see Supplementary Information).

4. *Greek tour.* Have students act as tour guides on a visit to Greece. Divide the task: have some students prepare brochures and others explain the itinerary.

5. *Homer.* Have students read and dramatize some scenes from adapted versions of the *Iliad* and *Odyssey.* (See the video *Homer's Mythology* in Resource Materials.)

Answer Key

page 229
Activity 1
Homer

page 231
Activity 2
A.

1. *gamma rays*—rays emitted by radioactive bodies, stronger than X rays

   Mississippi Delta—deposit of land at the mouth of the Mississippi River, shaped like a triangle, like the Greek letter delta

   I don't care one iota!—The word *iota* is the ninth letter of the Greek alphabet. It is used to refer to a very small amount. So the expression means "I don't care even a little bit."

   $A = \pi r^2$—The formula for the area of a circle. Area equals π (3.14) time the radius squared.

   Alpha to Omega—the same as saying from "A to Z" since alpha and omega are the first and last letters of the Greek alphabet.

2. *Phi Beta Kappa*—an honorary society, founded by Benjamin Franklin in 1776. Those receiving high grades in college are elected to this society.

   Sigma Chi, Alpha Zeta Delta—college social fraternities

B. Athens, Georgia or Ohio; Atlanta, Georgia; Ithaca, New York; Ypsilanti, Michigan

page 232
Activity 3
A. *Health Words:* dermatitis, dermatologist (dermat-, "skin"); osteopath, osteoporosis (oste, "bone"); cardiac, cardiologist (cardi-, "heart")
Technology Words: kilowatt, kilometer (kilo, "thousand"); heliport, helicopter (from *helix*, meaning "spiral"); telescope, telephone (tele-, "distant")
Science/Mathematics Words: polygon, polyglot (poly-, "many"); barometer, barometric (bar-, "pressure"); hydrogen, hydrofoil (hydro-, "water")

B.

1.
aer	air	*aerospace*
anthropos	human	anthropology
astron	*star*	astronomy
auto	self	*automatic*
bios	*life*	biology
ge	earth	*geology*
micros	*small*	microscope
phone	sound	telephone
theos	a god	theology
photon	light	*photograph*

3. cosmetology; ophthalmologist; zoology; geology; ornithologist

C.

1. *geography,* earth-writing (study of the earth); autograph, self-writing (e.g., writing one's name)

2. *telephone,* distant communication of sound on a special instrument; *telescope,* "far-seeing" instrument for space viewing; *telepathy,* distant communication by "feeling"; *telephoto,* "distant" light, a lens for photographing distant objects; *teletype,* a machine that types signals by either telegraph or telephone wires; *telecommunications,* science of electronic technology used for distant communication

3. *biology,* study of life; *zoology,* study of animals

4. *thermometer,* measure of heat; *pedometer,* measure of distance walked (from Latin *pes, pedis,* for "foot"; -*meter* is the Greek part)

page 236
Mystery Words
1. *school:* from Greek *skhole,* meaning "leisure"
2. The suffix -*crat* from *kratos,* meaning "strength, power." *Autocrat* is a person who has undisputed rule. *Plutocrat* is a member of a wealthy ruling class, from *ploutos,* meaning "wealth."

Fun Word
Tri- means "three"; *deka* means "ten"; *phobia* means "fear." This "fun" coined word, *triskaidekaphobia,* means fear of the number 13.

Supplementary Information

I. Egyptian Influence on Ancient Cultures

There is an increasing interest in the investigation of Greek connections with Egyptian civilization. In the multicultural classroom, as in any classroom, it is important to impart the sense of the *interrelationship* of civilizations. The Greeks did not emerge from a vacuum. This topic can be explored through these references: *African Presence in Early Europe,* edited by Ivan Von Sertima, Transaction Publishers (collection of essays including ones by Asa Hilliard and Edward Scobie) and *Blacks in Antiquity* by Frank M. Snowden, Jr., Harvard University Press, 1970. You might incorporate this material as appropriate into the study of ancient Greek.

II. Language Connections

A. Eureka!

Archimedes was an ancient Greek inventor and mathematician. *Eureka,* meaning "I have found it," was the word Archimedes is said to have shouted as he jumped out of his bathtub when he arrived at the solution to the question "Was the king's crown all gold?" ("Eureka" is the state motto of California.)

B. Story of Chlorophyll

Here are some examples of Greek roots being used to create scientific terminology.
chlorophyll:

> *chloros* = green, *phyllon* = leaf

oxygen = related to the Greek word "being born," hence sustaining life
photosynthesis:

> *photo* = relating to light

> *synthesis* = bringing together

C. *Arachnophobia*: A Hollywood Film
Arachnophobia:

> *arachne* = spider or web

> *phobia* = fear

So *arachnophobia* is a coined word meaning "fear of spiders."
Arachnids: a scientific name referring to spiders and scorpions (that have *eight* legs in contrast to insects, which have *six* legs). This name derives from a figure in classical mythology called *Arachne*, a young woman who challenged the goddess Athena to a weaving contest. Athena changed Arachne into a spider, hence the name. See also *Mini Page*, "Meet the Arthropods," July 22, 1990.

D. Dinosaur

Note that *dinosaur* names are also derived from ancient Greek. See *Mini Page*, "Dinosaurs from A to Z," May 26, 1991.

III. Modern Greek

You might want to present these modern Greek expressions to the class. You might also want to get some simple language learning tapes for pronunciation help.

A. Greetings

Introduce students to the following expressions in modern Greek:
[set Greek attached, in third column]

English	**How It Sounds**	**Greek**
good morning	kahlee*meh*rah	Καλημερα
hello, good-bye	yi*a*ssoo	Γει ασου
How are you?	ti *kah*nees	Τι κανεις?
Very well, thanks	po*lee* kah*lah*,	Πολυ καλα,
	ehfkahree*sto*	ευχαριστω
Good afternoon	kahlee*sp*erah	Καλησπερα
Good night	kahlee*neek*tah	Καληνυχτα

Have them practice exchanging greetings.

B. Numbers

	How It Sounds	Greek
0	*meethehn* (*th* as in *mother*)	μηδεν
1	*en*nah	ενα
2	*theeo* (*th* as in *mother*)	δυο
3	*tree*ah	τρια
4	*teh*seerah	τεσσερα
5	*pehn*deh	πεντε
6	*ehk*see	εξι
7	ehp*tah*	επτα
8	ok*to*	οκτω
9	ehnee*ah*	εννια
10	*then*kah (*th* as in *mother*)	δεκα

Resource Materials

Note: For addresses of publishers and distributors, refer to Appendix A, Master Address List.

Teacher Reference

Books

English from the Roots Up, 1990. Available from the American Classical League (Includes Greek roots and their English derivatives)

Women in Ancient Greece and Rome, by Michael Massey, Cambridge University Press, 1988.

World Mythology, National Textbook, by Donna Rosenberg, 1986.

Language Materials

Greek for Travelers, Berlitz. (Accompanying tape useful for help in pronouncing modern Greek)

Pamphlets

Culturgram for Greece, Center for International Studies, Brigham Young University. (For modern Greece)

Class Materials

I. Student Magazine

Calliope, Cobblestone Publishing. (Articles and projects about Roman and Greek history, archaeology, games, word origins)

II. Videos/Filmstrips

The Greeks and the Romans, Knowledge Unlimited. (Filmstrip/video, with teacher guide)

Homer's Mythology, Guidance Associates.

Mythology: Gods and Goddesses, Guidance Associates.

Mythology Is Alive and Well, Guidance Associates. (Relating mythology to modern world such as in science fiction, rock music)

III. Posters

Available from the American Classical League are these: Greek wall alphabet chart, Greek mythology posters, Scientific Inventions Chart (Greek and Latin sources of scientific names), Atomic Age Poster (Greek and Latin sources of terms)
    Available from Knowledge Unlimited: Ancient Civilizations Poster Set (Greeks)
    Available from Social Studies School Service: travel posters

IV. Wall Maps/Desk Maps

Available from Rand McNally

V. Realia

Available from Bolchazy-Carducci Publishing: badges with Eureka in Greek letters

Available from Claudia's Caravan: "All One People" buttons in Greek

VI. Cooking Experiences

Cooking the Greek Way, Lerner Publications, 1984.

VII. Songs

Mythology Songbook, American Classical League. (Musical versions of familiar myths using well-known tunes)

VIII. Activities

Ancient Greece, Civilization Project Book, Franklin Watts, 1982. (Hands-on activities)

Coloring Book of Ancient Greece, Bellerophon Books.

Coloring Book of the Olympic Games, Bellerophon Books.

Costumes of the Greeks and Romans, Dover Publishing. (Reproducible pages)

Themes for Classical Studies, by Ashley Carter et al., Cambridge University Press, 1991. (Reproducible maps, worksheets about ancient Greece and Rome)

IX. Multicultural Background Reading

The Ancient Olympic Games, American Classical League.

Greece, by Bridgett and Neil Ardley, Silver Burdett, 1989.

Greeks in America, Lerner Publications, 1987.

Mythology and You, by Donna Rosenberg, National Textbook, 1992.

Usborne Illustrated Guide to Greek Myths and Legends, by Cheryl Evans and Anne Millard, (Usborne) EDC Publishers, 1986. (Includes glossary of "Who's Who in Greek Mythology")

Welcome to Ancient Greece, by Anne Millard, National Textbook, 1981.

Ye Gods!, by Helen Britt, Longman, 1987. (About Greek and Roman mythology)

What's in a Word?, by David Zaslow, Good Apple, 1983. (For information on Greek derivatives)

Useful Addresses

American Classical League
Miami University
Oxford, OH 45056
(Main source of teaching materials for ancient Greek and Greece)

National Greek Tourist Organization
645 Fifth Ave.
New York, NY 10022
(Photographs, brochures about Greek landmarks)

Appendix A

MASTER ADDRESS LIST

This list includes the addresses of the publishers and distributors mentioned in the Resource Materials.

Alfred Knopf
(see Random House)

American Classical League
Miami University
Oxford, OH 45056

American Forum
Suite 908
45 John St.
New York, NY 10038

Applause Learning Resources
85A Fernwood Lane
Roslyn, NY 11576

Asia Society
725 Park Ave.
New York, NY 10021

Association for Supervision and
Curriculum Development
1250 N. Pitt St.
Alexandria, VA 22314

Atheneum Publishers
(see Macmillan)

Audio Forum
96 Broad St.
Guilford, CT 06437

Aylmer Press
P.O. Box 2735
Madison, WI 53701

Baker & Taylor Books
50 Kirby
Somerville, NJ 08876

Barclay School Supplies
166 Livingston St.
Brooklyn, NY 11201

Bellerophon Books
36 Anacapa St.
Santa Barbara, CA 93101

Berlitz Publications
257 Park Ave. S.
New York, NY 10022

Bess Press
P.O. Box 22388
Honolulu, HI 96823

Bilingual Books, Inc.
6018 Seaview Ave, NW
Seattle, WA 98107

Blackwood Press
P.O. Box 11511
Atlanta, GA 30310

Bolchazy-Carducci
Suite 101
1000 Brown St.
Wauconda, IL 60084

Bookwright Press
387 Park Ave. South
New York, NY 10016

Brigham Young University
Center for International Studies
Provo, UT 84602

Cambridge University Press
40 W. Twentieth St.
New York, NY 10011

Carol Rhoda Books, Inc.
First Ave. North
Minneapolis, MN 55401

Chelsea House
300 Park Ave.
New York, NY 10016

Childrens Press
c/o Grolier
5444 N. Cumberland Ave.
Chicago, IL 60656

Chinese Historical Society of
America
17 Adler Place
San Francisco, CA 94133

Chronicle Books
275 Fifth Ave.
San Francisco, CA 94103

Claudia's Caravan
1918 Lafayette St.
Alameda, CA 94501

Cobblestone Publishing Company
30 Grove St.
Peterborough, NH 03458

College Board
888 Seventh Ave.
New York, NY 10106

Continental Press, Inc.
520 E. Bainbridge St.
Elizabethtown, PA 17022

Coward-McCann, Inc.
(see G. P. Putnam's)

Thomas Crowell Junior Books
10 E. Fifty-Third St.
New York, NY 10022

Crabtree Publishers
350 Fifth Ave. Suite 3308
New York, NY 10118

Cultural Connections
(see Claudia's Caravan)

Delta Systems
1400 Miller Pkwy.
McHenry, IL 60050

Dial Books for Young Readers
375 Hudson St.
New York, NY 10014
or
Box 120 (orders)
Bergenfield, NJ 07261

Dillon Press, Inc.
(see Macmillan)

Donovan Music and Toy
Waukesha, WI 53186

Doubleday
(Bantam, Doubleday, Dell)
666 Fifth Ave.
New York, NY 10103

Dover Publications
31 East Second St.
Mineola, NY 11501

Dufour Editions
P.O. Box 7
Chester Springs, PA 19425

Educational Extension Systems
P.O. Box 259
Clark's Summit, PA 18411

EDC Publishers
8141 E. Forty-Fourth St.
Tulsa, OK 74145

EMC Corporation
300 York Ave.
Saint Paul, MN 55101

Enslow Publishers
Bloy St. and Ramsey Ave.
Box 777
Hillside, NJ 07205

Esperanto League for North
　America
P.O. Box 1129
El Cerrito, CA 94530

Farrar, Straus & Giroux
19 Union Square West
New York, NY 10003

Franklin Watts, Inc.
5444 N. Cumberland Ave.
Chicago, IL 60656

W. H. Freeman & Company
41 Madison Ave.
New York, NY 10010
or
4419 W. 1980 St. (orders)
Salt Lake City, UT 84104

French for Fun
Suite 224
1700 Ygnacio Valley Rd.
Walnut, CA 94598

Gessler Publishing Company
55 W. Thirteenth St.
New York, NY 10011

Globe Book Company
4350 Equity Dr.
P.O. Box 2649
Columbus, OH 43216

Goethe Institute
1014 Fifth Ave.
New York, NY 10028

Good Apple, Inc.
1204 Buchanan St.
P.O. Box 299
Carthage, IL 62321

Greenhaven Press, Inc.
P.O. Box 289009
San Diego, CA 92198

Greenwood Press
(Greenwood Publishing Group)
88 Post Rd., W. Box 5007
Westport, CT 06881

Guidance Associates
P.O. Box 1000
Mt. Kisco, NY 10549

Harcourt Brace Jovanovich
6277 Sea Harbor Dr.
Orlando, FL 32887

HarperCollins Publishers
10 E. Fifty-Third St.
New York, NY 10022

Harvard University
Center for Middle Eastern Studies
Cambridge, MA 02138

Henry Holt, Inc.
115 W. Eighteenth St.
New York, NY 10011

Holmes & Meier Publishing
　Company
30 Irving St.
New York, NY 10003

Houghton Mifflin
Wayside Rd.
Burlington, MA 01803

International Book Centre
P.O. Box 295
Troy, MI 48099

JACP, Inc.
414 East Third Ave.
San Mateo, CA 94401

Johns Hopkins University
School of Advanced International
　Studies
1740 Massachusetts Ave., NW
Washington, DC 20036

The Kiosk
19223 DeHavilland Dr.
Saratoga, CA 95070

Knowledge Unlimited
Box 52
Madison, WI 53701

Kodansha
114 Fifth Ave.
New York, NY 10011

The Learning Works, Inc.
P.O. Box 6187
Santa Barbara, CA 93160

Lerner Publications
241 First Ave. North
Minneapolis, MN 55401

Library of Nations
(see Silver Burdett)

Lingo Fun, Inc.
P.O. Box 486
Westerville, OH 43081

J. P. Lippincott
227 E. Washington Square
Philadelphia, PA 19106

Little, Brown & Co.
34 Beacon St.
Boston, MA 02108

Longman Publishing Group
10 Bank St.
White Plains, NY 10606

Macmillan Publishing Co.
866 Third Ave.
New York, NY 10022
(also for Macmillan Child Group)

Mainline Publishing Co.
P.O. Box 914
Suite 400
1974 Sproul Rd.
Broomall, PA 19008

McDougal, Littell
P.O. Box 1667
Evanston, IL 60204

Middle East Studies Association
Department of Oriental Studies
University of Arizona
Tucson, AZ 85721

Mini Page
P.O. Box 419150
Kansas City, MO 64141

William Morrow & Company
1350 Avenue of the Americas
New York, NY 10019

National Geographic Society
Educational Services
1145 Seventeenth St., NW
Washington, DC 20036

National Museum of African Art
Smithsonian Institution
950 Independence Ave, SW
Washington, DC 20560

National Textbook Company
4255 W. Touhy Ave.
Lincolnwood, IL 60646

Northeast Conference on Teaching
   Foreign Languages
200 Twin Oaks Terrace #16
South Burlington, VT 06400

W. W. Norton Publishers
500 Fifth Ave.
New York, NY 10110

Oxford University Press
200 Madison Ave.
New York, NY 10016

Passport Books
(see National Textbook)

Penguin
(see Viking)

Picaflor Productions
6109 Wilmett Road
Betheseda, MD 20817

Place-in-the World Publishing
3900 Glenwood Ave.
Golden Valley, MN 55422

Prentice-Hall
Route 9W
Englewood, NJ 07632

Prentice-Hall Press
(see Simon & Schuster)

Publishers Choice
Box 4171
Dept. DF10-PD
Huntington Station, NY 11746

G. P. Putnam's
Putnam Publishing Group
200 Madison Ave.
New York, NY 10016

Rand McNally
8255 Central Park Ave.
Skokie, IL 60076

Random House
201 E. Fifieth St.
New York, NY 10022
or
400 Hahn Rd. (orders)
Westminster, MD 21157

Rounders Records
42-15 Crescent St.
Long Island City, NY 11101

Routledge, Chapman & Hall
29 W. Thirty-Fifth St.
New York, NY 10001

Scholars Press
P.O. Box 15399
Atlanta, GA 30333

Scholastic, Inc.
730 Broadway
New York, NY 10003

Charles Scribner's Sons
597 Fifth Ave.
New York, NY 10017

St. Martin's Press
175 Fifth Ave.
New York, NY 10010

Silver Burdett
Unit of Simon & Schuster
   Elementary
250 James St.
Morristown, NJ 07960
(also Library of Nations)

Simon & Schuster
200 Old Tappan Rd. (orders)
Old Tappan, NJ 07675
(also Prentice-Hall Press)

Society for Visual Education
   (SVE)
1345 W. Diversey Pkwy.
Chicago, IL 60614

Social Sciences Education
   Consortium, Inc.
3300 Mitchell Lane
Boulder, CO 80301

Social Studies School Service
10200 Jefferson Blvd. Room Y9
P.O. Box 802
Culver City, CA 90232

Steck-Vaughn
Box 26015
Austin, TX 78755

Teacher's Discovery
1000 Owendale, Suite H
Box 7048
Troy, MI 48007

Time-Life
Box 2649
Columbus, OH 43216

Touch and See
P.O. Box 794
Palos Verdes Estates, CA 90274

Charles E. Tuttle Company
Rutland, VT 05701

Viking Press
Division of Penguin
375 Hudson St.
New York, NY 10014

Villard Press
(see Random House)

Wellness Reproductions, Inc.
Suite 6
23945 Mercantile Dr.
Beachwood, OH 44122

Western Publishing Company,
   Inc.
2020 Maund Ave.
Racine, WI 53404

World Awareness, Inc.
890 Twin Towers
Ypsilanti, MI 48198

World Press
135 W. Twenty-Ninth St.
New York, NY 10001

Appendix B

COURSE PRETEST
AND POSTTEST

Pretest on Language and Cultural Concepts

Directions: Based on your knowledge, decide whether each statement is true or false. Write *T* for *True* or *F* for *False*.

_____ 1. Language is a system of sounds.

_____ 2. Modern languages change all the time.

_____ 3. Languages are completely different. None are related in any way.

_____ 4. All languages use an alphabet.

_____ 5. Knowing languages is useful only to people who want to work in foreign countries.

_____ 6. Many English prefixes like *pre-* and *post-* come from Latin.

_____ 7. All alphabets have twenty-six letters.

_____ 8. Languages differ in how they are put together.

_____ 9. *Breakfast* means the same in all countries.

_____ 10. English has borrowed words from other languages.

Posttest on Language and Cultural Concepts

Directions: Below are ten statements of some general ideas from your Exploratory Language course. Using what you learned in the course, decide whether each statement is true or false. Write *T* for *True* or *F* for *False*.

_____ 1. You can express ideas with and without words.

_____ 2. Some languages use symbols for words and do not use an alphabet.

_____ 3. English is a Romance language.

_____ 4. Languages borrow words and expressions from one another.

_____ 5. The word *hello* is used in all languages.

_____ 6. German, French, and Spanish belong to the same large *branch* of human languages called Indo-European.

_____ 7. Languages usually have expressions for greeting people.

_____ 8. Languages are usually spoken in only one country.

_____ 9. English has many prefixes and roots from Latin.

_____ 10. English is the same as it was one thousand years ago.

Answers:

Pretest	Posttest
Pretest	**Posttest**
1. T	1. T
2. T	2. T
3. F	3. F
4. F	4. T
5. F	5. F
6. T	6. T
7. F	7. T
8. T	8. F
9. F	9. T
10. T	10. F

Student Activity Pages

Answer Key

Copies or transparencies of these pages may
be made for classroom use.

Chapter 2   Signs and Symbols

EXPERIENCE ESPERANTO

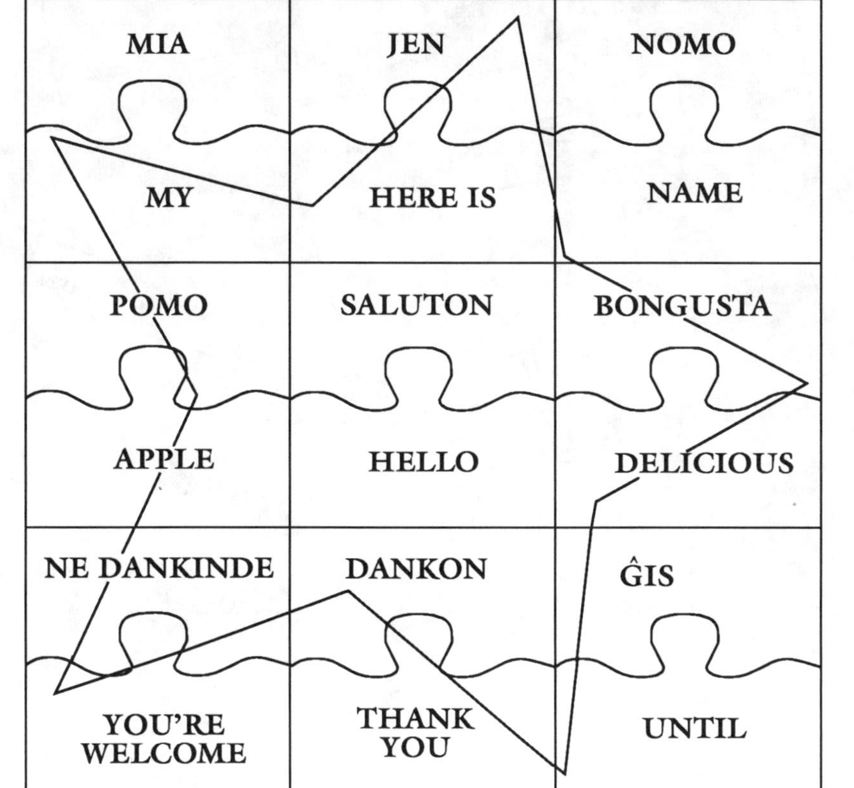

Directions:
1. Cut out the puzzle pieces with the English words on Sheet 2.
2. Match the cut-out pieces by pasting them below their Esperanto equivalents on Sheet 1.
Use the lines on the pieces as a guide.
3. The completed puzzle shows a star, the Esperanto symbol.

Chapter 3   Your Language and Mine

STATES

Write the number of the original name next to the current name of each of the U.S. states below.

1.	alibamos	ALABAMA	1
2.	ouisconsing	ALASKA	14
3.	ouaricon	ARIZONA	12
4.	eedahhow	CONNECTICUT	6
5.	kentake	DAKOTA	11
6.	quonoktacut	IDAHO	4
7.	tanasse	ILLINOIS	8
8.	iliniwek	KENTUCKY	5
9.	ahioha	MICHIGAN	10
10.	mishiguma	MISSISSIPPI	15
11.	lahkota	OHIO	9
12.	arizonaca	OREGON	3
13.	ute	TENNESSEE	7
14.	alayeska	TEXAS	16
15.	maesisipu	UTAH	13
16.	tejas	WISCONSIN	2

THE WAY THEY WERE

Chapter 4　Families of Languages

Use a large dictionary or an encyclopedia to find the name of the language family that each language below belongs to. Write the name of the family on the line marked **FROM**.

Chapter 5　Exploring Spanish and the Hispanic World

RHYMING TIME

Complete the poem with words relating to Spanish culture and language. At times, there may be several possible answers. (You'll find the Spanish words you need in Chapter 5 of your book.) (Possible answers are given.)

Here's a poem just for you,
So fill it out with much **gusto**.
As the Spanish world you explore,
Increase your knowledge more and more.

Some countries where they say *¡hola!*
Are **Spain, Mexico, Venezuela**, and **Colombia**.
Hispanic place names, you might guess
Are **San Antonio** and **Los Angeles** here in the U.S.
We've even borrowed Spanish words, you know,
Like **burro, bolero, piñata**, and **taco**.

Counting in Spanish you can do *pronto*
With numbers like **tres, quatro**, and **cinco**.
To say what day of the week you face,
You may use **lunes, martes**, or **miércoles**.
If the months of the year are confusing,
marzo, abril, or **mayo** you should be using.

Greeting a **señor** or *señora* today,
hola and **buenos días** you would say.
And when your friends have to go,
Say good-bye with **adiós** or **hasta luego**.
"What's your name?" would be **¿Come se llama?**
Answer with names like **María** and **Ana**.

As you widen your horizons without end,
Spanish language and culture are your **amigos**, your friends.

Chapter 6 Exploring French and the French-Speaking World

On parle français

WORD FIND

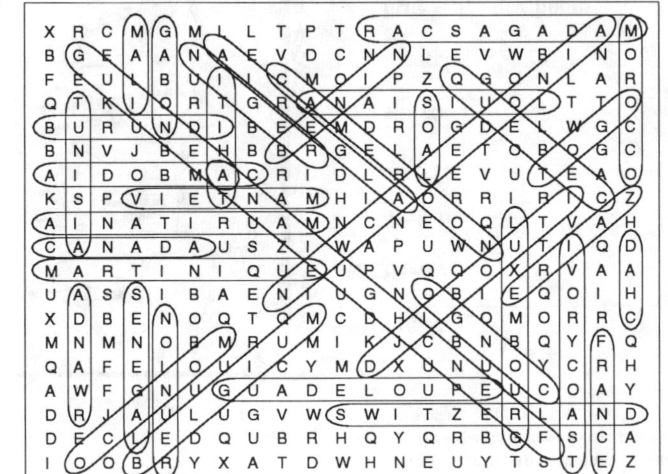

New Caledonia	French Guiana	Switzerland	Luxembourg
Ivory Coast	Guadeloupe	Madagascar	Martinique
Mauritania	Louisiana	Cameroon	Djibouti
Cambodia	Algeria	Morocco	Belgium
Reunion	Senegal	Vietnam	Tunisia
Burundi	Quebec	Canada	Tahiti
France	Benin	Gabon	Zaire
Togo	Congo	Niger	Laos
Chad	Mali		

Chapter 7 Exploring German and German-Speaking Areas

MEIN NAME IST

FRITZ

Complete this chart referring to *A Story in German* in the textbook.

	GERMAN	ENGLISH
1.	**Name**	name
2.	Familie	**family**
3.	Deutschland	**Germany**
4.	**Vater**	father
5.	**Mutter**	mother
6.	Englisch	**English**
7.	**Schule**	school
8.	Bruder	**brother**
9.	**Schwester**	sister
10.	Universität	**university**

Chapter 8   Exploring Italian, Italy, and Its People

USE YOUR NOODLE

Use a cookbook or a dictionary or talk to someone who speaks Italian to find the meaning of each of these pasta names. Write the meaning on the line.

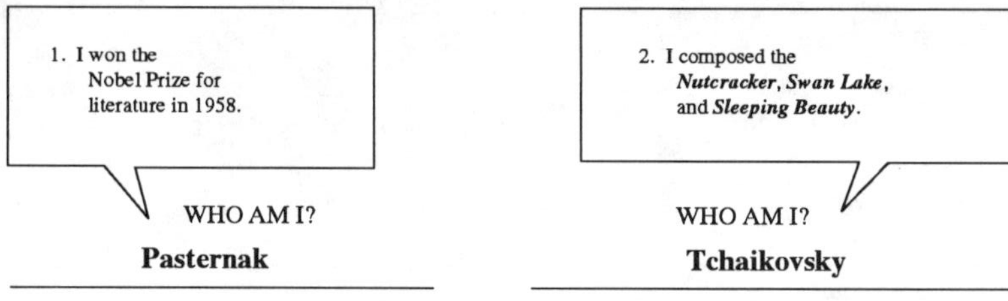

1. spaghetti

    little stings

2. linguine

    little tongues

3. manicotti

    sleeves

4. fettuccine

    little strips or ribbons

5. rigatoni

    lined tubes

6. rotini

    little wheels

7. ravioli

    little turnips

8. vermicelli

    little worms

Chapter 9   Exploring Russian, Russia, and Its People

NOTABLE RUSSIANS

1. I won the Nobel Prize for literature in 1958.

WHO AM I?
Pasternak

2. I composed the *Nutcracker*, *Swan Lake*, and *Sleeping Beauty*.

WHO AM I?
Tchaikovsky

3. I am the leader who founded the Communist government in Russia.

WHO AM I?
Lenin

4. I am the Russian novelist who wrote *War and Peace.*

WHO AM I?
Tolstoy

5. I was the first czar of Russia.

WHO AM I?
Ivan the Terrible

6. I wrote the music for *Peter and the Wolf.*

WHO AM I?
Prokofiev

7. I am the "on again, off again" Russian city. What is my name today?

WHAT CITY AM I?
St. Petersburg

8. I had the Winter Palace built.

WHO AM I?
Catherine the Great

RUSSIAN NOTABLES

Chapter 10 Exploring Japanese, Japan, and Its People

CAPTURE QUEST

Cross out the incorrect letters to reveal the mystery words. When you finish, copy the letters that have a number below them in the correct blanks at the bottom of the activity.

1. "good-bye" in Japanese

B̶ S P̶ A Y O̶ I̶ W N A R A
   3   5

2. mound of rice with raw fish, seaweed, or vegetables

Ø̶ R̶ S U A̶ T̶ S P̶ H I P̶A̶
          8

3. straw mat to cover the floor

T D̶ A F̶ T̶ H A̶ I̶ M L̶ I Y̶
         4

4. Japanese "thank you"

A B̶ R Y̶ I K̶ G L̶ A R̶ T O
         6

5. Japanese robe

S̶ K X̶ I Z M C̶ O G̶ N I̶ O
   2   9

6. salad in Japanese

H̶ S Ø̶ A R T̶ A K D I̶ A̶
     7   1

COMPLETE THE SENTENCE:

Japan is known as the Land of the

$$\frac{R}{1}\ \frac{I}{2}\ \frac{S}{3}\ \frac{I}{4}\ \frac{N}{5}\ \frac{G}{6}$$

$$\frac{S}{7}\ \frac{U}{8}\ \frac{N}{9}$$

Chapter 11 Exploring Chinese, China, and Its People

GREAT WALL

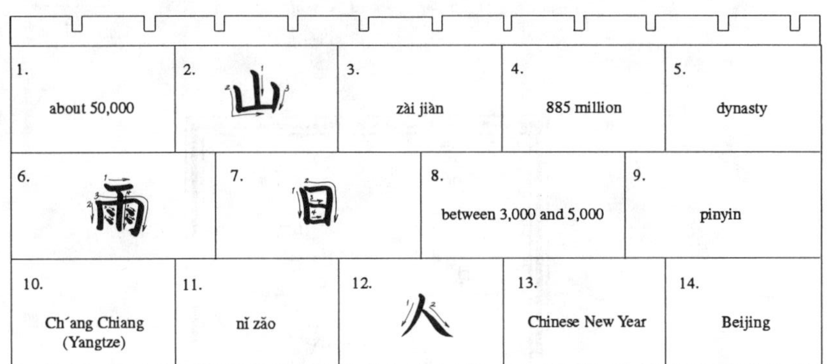

1.	2.	3.	4.	5.
about 50,000	山	zài jiàn	885 million	dynasty
6. 雨	7. 日	8. between 3,000 and 5,000		9. pinyin
10. Ch´ang Chiang (Yangtze)	11. nǐ zǎo	12. 人	13. Chinese New Year	14. Beijing

Complete the wall by filling in the blocks.
Each block should contain the response to the numbered clues:

1. number of characters in Chinese

2. draw the Chinese character for *mountain*

3. pinyin spelling for *good-bye*

4. number of people who speak Mandarin Chinese

5. period of time when emperors of the same family ruled

6. draw the Chinese character for *rain*

7. draw the Chinese character for *sun*

8. number of characters an average Chinese person knows

9. system that aids in pronunciation ("spell sound")

10. the great river that flows through China

11. pinyin spelling for *good morning*

12. draw the Chinese character for *person*

13. Chinese holiday in late January or early February

14. capital of China

Chapter 12 Exploring Arabic and the Arabic-Speaking World

ANSWER IN ARABIC

Read the questions and situations in the box below. How would you respond to them in Arabic?
Put the letter of each situation next to the appropriate Arabic response to it.

A. Your friend from Algeria gave you some baklawa.

B. Arabic is read left to right like English. Yes or No?

C. You encounter a friend on a street in Cairo.

D. The number of letters in the Arabic alphabet is 28.

E. You open the door and invite your friend from Oman into your home.

F. The Arabic alphabet is the most widely used in the world. Yes or No?

G. You are wondering how a friend is feeling.

H. You are taking leave of your friend.

E	1.	أهلا و سهلا	(ahlan wa-sahlan)
G	2.	كيف حالك؟	(keef halak)
C	3.	السلام عليكم	(as-salaam alaykom)
H	4.	مع السلامة	(maa al salaama)
D	5.	نعم	(naam)
B, F	6.	لا	(la)
A	7.	شكرا	(shookran)

Chapter 13 Exploring the Hebrew Language, Israel, and Its People

WHAT DO YOU KNOW ABOUT ISRAEL AND THE HEBREW LANGUAGE?

Answer with

כֵּן.
(ken)

yes

or

לֹא.
(lo)

no

ken	1. "Shalom" means "peace," "hello," and "good-bye."
ken	2. The Hebrew alphabet has twenty-two consonants.
lo	3. Shabbat is a unit of money in Israel.
lo	4. The two official languages of Israel are Hebrew and English.
ken	5. Israel used to be called Palestine.
ken	6. The Hebrew language is two thousand years old.
ken	7. In a kibbutz, everyone shares things equally.
ken	8. The Hebrew calendar is based on the cycles of the moon.
lo	9. Israel became an independent country four thousand years ago.
ken	10. Rosh Hashanah and Yom Kippur are important Jewish holidays.

Chapter 14   Exploring Swahili and Swahili- Speaking Areas

SWAHILI SECRET MESSAGE

Look at the English clues in the box below, and fill in the crossword puzzles with the corresponding Swahili expressions. Complete the puzzle, and a secret message will be revealed.

Puzzle 1 (answers filled in):

- 1. h a p a n a
- 2. s i k i t u
- 3. m o j a
- 4. a s a n t e
- 5. k u m i
- 6. m b i l i
- 7. n d i y o

Puzzle 2 (answers filled in):

- 8. s a b a
- 9. k w a n z a a
- 10. h r a a m b e
- 11. u h u r u
- 12. k w a h e r i
- 13. u h a l i g a n i
- 14. t i s a

Across
1. no
2. you're welcome
3. one
4. thank you
5. ten
6. two
7. yes
8. seven
9. harvest
10. together
11. freedom
12. good-bye
13. How are you?
14. nine

Chapter 15   Exploring Latin, Ancient Rome, and Its People

Latin in Our Language

Look at the *English word* in the left-hand column. Fill in the meaning of the *English word* in the middle column. Then, write the related Latin word in the right-hand column. Use a dictionary to help you find the answers.

	MEANING OF ENGLISH WORDS	LATIN
1. *amicable* relations	*friendly*	*amicus*
2. the town's *centennial* celebration	hundredth anniversary	centum
3. *gratifying* to hear	pleasing	gratias
4. a *stellar* performance	related to the stars, brilliant	stella
5. a *lunar* expedition	related to the moon	luna
6. the *quartet* of singers	a group of four	quattuor
7. *uniquely* the first number	only one of its kind	unus
8. the salesperson's *territory*	land or area	terra

**Chapter 16 Exploring Greek, Greece, and
the Ancient Greek World**

GETTING TO THE ROOT
OF GREEK

Draw a simple sketch or symbol that expresses the meaning of each Greek word part. In the spaces,
write three English words that contain that part. Use a dictionary if you need help.
Possible answers:

bio-	metr-	hydro-	tele-
biology	metric	hydroelectric	telephone
biochemistry	meter	hydrogen	telegraph
biosphere	metronome	hydrofoil	television

graph-	astron-	geo-	photo-
graphics	astronomy	geology	photograph
graphology	astronomer	geography	photosynthesis
graph	astronaut	geocentric	photon

Appendix D

Student Activity Pages

Name ___________________________________ Date ___________________

EXPERIENCE ESPERANTO

MIA	JEN	NOMO
POMO	SALUTON	BONGUSTA
NE DANKINDE	DANKON	ĜIS

Directions:

1. Cut out the puzzle pieces with the English words on Sheet 2.

2. Match the cut-out pieces by pasting them below their Esperanto equivalents on Sheet 1.
   Use the lines on the pieces as a guide.

3. The completed puzzle shows a star, the Esperanto symbol.

Name _______________________________________ Date _______________

THANK YOU
APPLE
YOU'RE WELCOME
UNTIL
HERE IS
DELICIOUS
MY
HELLO
NAME

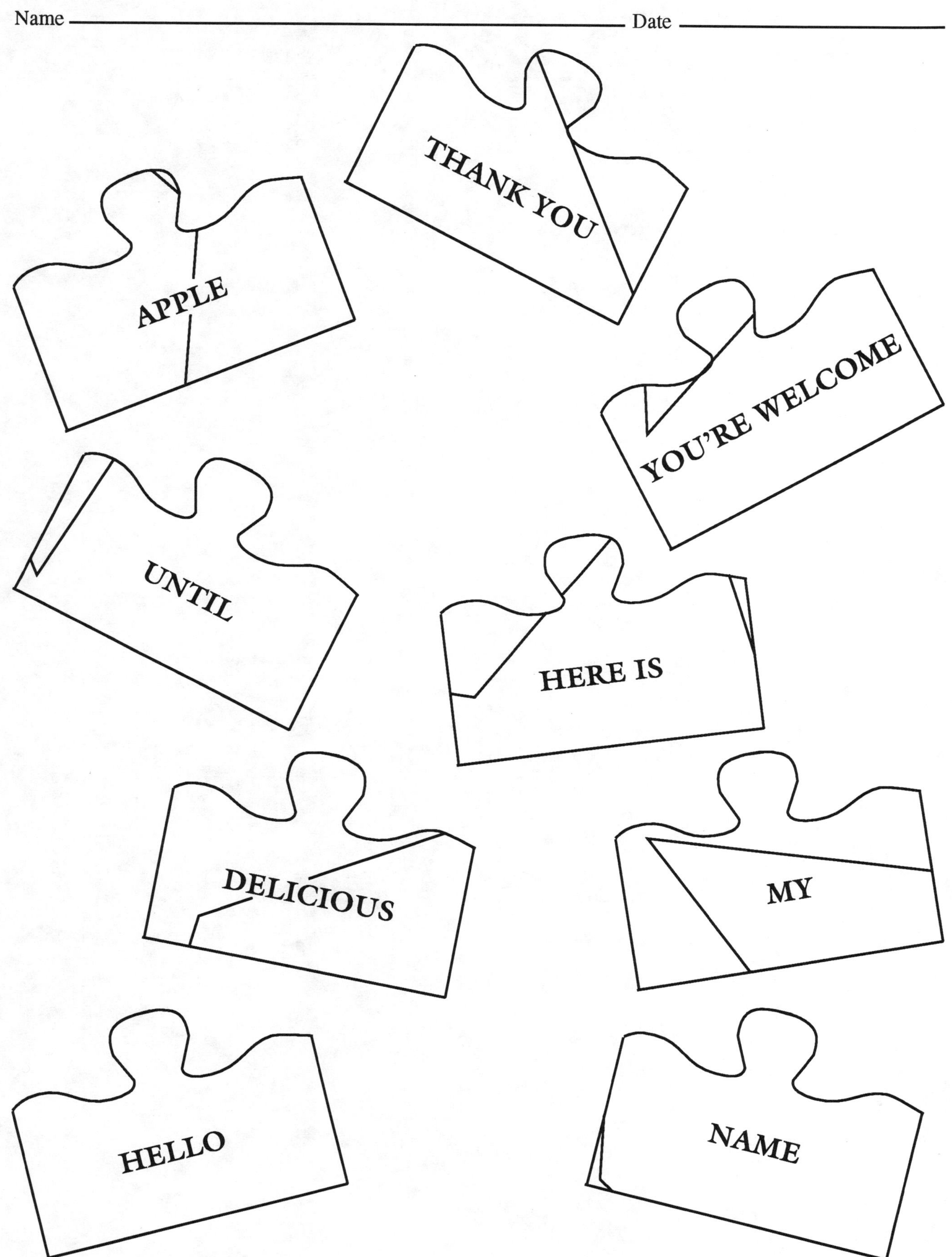

Name _______________________________________ Date _______________________________

STATES

Write the number of the original name next to the current name of each of the U.S. states below.

1. alibamos
2. ouisconsing
3. ouaricon
4. eedahhow
5. kentake
6. quonoktacut
7. tanasse
8. iliniwek
9. ahioha
10. mishiguma
11. lahkota
12. arizonaca
13. ute
14. alayeska
15. maesisipu
16. tejas

ALABAMA _____
ALASKA _____
ARIZONA _____
CONNECTICUT _____
DAKOTA _____
IDAHO _____
ILLINOIS _____
KENTUCKY _____
MICHIGAN _____
MISSISSIPPI _____
OHIO _____
OREGON _____
TENNESSEE _____
TEXAS _____
UTAH _____
WISCONSIN _____

THE WAY THEY WERE

Name —————————————————————————— Date ——————————

Use a large dictionary or an encyclopedia to find the name of the language family that each language below belongs to. Write the name of the family on the line marked **FROM**.

Name ____ Date _________________

RHYMING TIME

Complete the poem with words relating to Spanish culture and language. At times, there may be several possible answers. (You'll find the Spanish words you need in Chapter 5 of your book.)

Here's a poem just for you,

So fill it out with much g_____________.

As the Spanish world you explore,

Increase your knowledge more and more.

Some countries where they say *¡hola!*

Are _______________, _______________, _______________, and _____________a.

Hispanic place names, you might guess

Are _______________ and _______________ here in the U.S.

We've even borrowed Spanish words, you know,

Like _______________, _______________, _______________, and _______________o.

Counting in Spanish you can do *pronto*

With numbers like _______________, _______________, and _______________o.

To say what day of the week you face,

You may use _______________, _______________, or _______________es.

If the months of the year are confusing,

_______________, _______________, or _______________ you should be using.

Greeting a _______________ or *señora* today,

_______________ and _______________ you would say.

And when your friends have to go,

Say good-bye with _______________ or _______________o.

"What's your name?" would be ¿_______________________________________?

Answer with names like _______________ and _______________a.

As you widen your horizons without end,

Spanish language and culture are your _______________, your friends.

Name____ Date_____________________

On parle français

WORD FIND

```
X R C M G M L L T P T R A C S A G A D A M
B G E A A N A E V D C N N L E V W B I N O
F E U L B U I I C M O I P Z Q G O N L A R
Q T K I O R T G R A N A I S I U O L T T O
B U R U N D I B E E M D R O G D E L W G C
B N V J B E H B B R G E L A E T O B O G C
A I D O B M A C R I D L R L E V U T E A O
K S P V I E T N A M H I A O R R I R I C Z
A I N A T I R U A M N C N E O Q L T V A H
C A N A D A U S Z I W A P U W N U T I Q D
M A R T I N I Q U E U P V Q Q O X R V A A
U A S S I B A E N I U G N O B I E Q O I H
X D B E N O Q T Q M C D H I G O M O R R C
M N M N O B M R U M I K J C B N B Q Y F Q
Q A F E I O U I C Y M D X U N U O Y C R H
A W F G N U G U A D E L O U P E U C O A Y
D R J A U L U G V W S W I T Z E R L A N D
D E C L E D Q U B R H Q Y Q R B G F S C A
I O O B R Y X A T D W H N E U Y T S T E Z
```

New Caledonia	French Guiana	Switzerland	Luxembourg
Ivory Coast	Guadeloupe	Madagascar	Martinique
Mauritania	Louisiana	Cameroon	Djibouti
Cambodia	Algeria	Morocco	Belgium
Reunion	Senegal	Vietnam	Tunisia
Burundi	Quebec	Canada	Tahiti
France	Benin	Gabon	Zaire
Togo	Congo	Niger	Laos
Chad	Mali		

Name _______________________________________ Date _______________

MEIN NAME IST

FRITZ

Complete this chart referring to *A Story in German* in the textbook.

	GERMAN	ENGLISH
1.		name
2.	Familie	
3.	Deutschland	
4.		father
5.		mother
6.	Englisch	
7.		school
8.	Bruder	
9.		sister
10.	Universität	

Name ___________________________________   Date ___________________

USE YOUR NOODLE

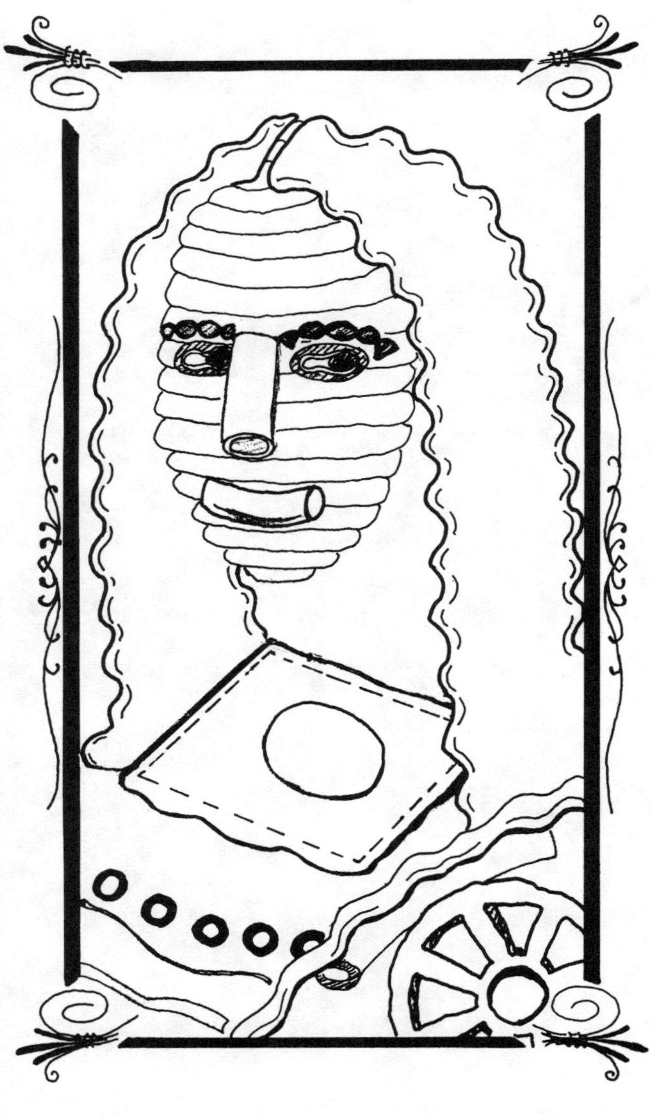

Use a cookbook or a dictionary or talk to some-one who speaks Italian to find the meaning of each of these pasta names. Write the meaning on the line.

1. spaghetti

____

2. linguine

____

3. manicotti

____

4. fettuccine

____

5. rigatoni

____

6. rotini

____

7. ravioli

____

8. vermicelli

____

Name ______________________________ Date ______________

NOTABLE RUSSIANS

1. I won the
Nobel Prize for
literature in 1958.

WHO AM I?

____

2. I composed the
Nutcracker, *Swan Lake*,
and *Sleeping Beauty*.

WHO AM I?

____

3. I am the leader
who founded the
Communist govern-
ment in Russia.

WHO AM I?

____

4. I am the
Russian novelist
who wrote
War and Peace.

WHO AM I?

5. I was the
first czar
of Russia.

WHO AM I?

____

6. I wrote the
music for
*Peter and
the Wolf.*

WHO AM I?

7. I am the "on again,
off again" Russian city.
What is my name today?

WHAT CITY AM I?

8. I had the
Winter
Palace
built.

WHO AM I?

____

RUSSIAN NOTABLES

Name ____ Date ___________________

CAPTURE QUEST

Cross out the incorrect letters to reveal the mystery words. When you finish, copy the letters that have a number below them in the correct blanks at the bottom of the activity.

1. "good-bye" in Japanese

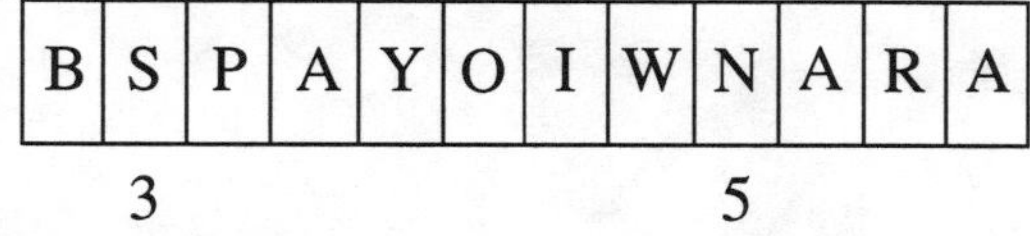

2. mound of rice with raw fish, seaweed, or vegetables

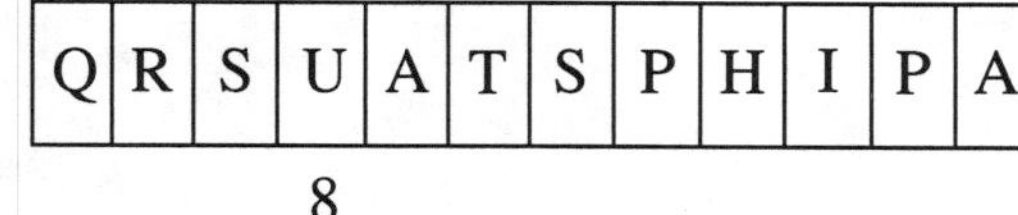

3. straw mat to cover the floor

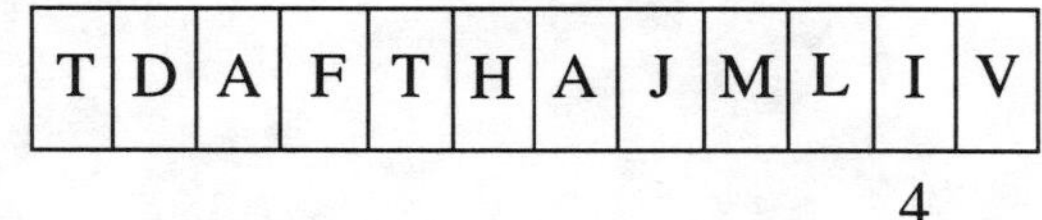

4. Japanese "thank you"

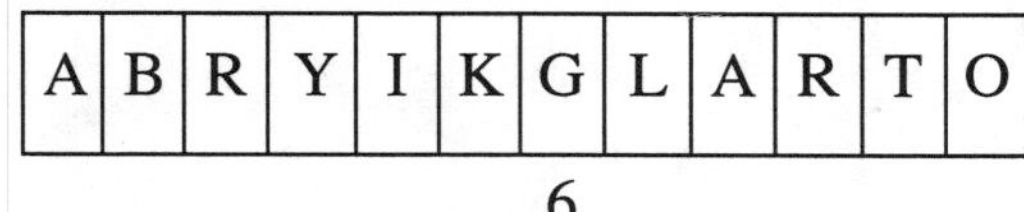

5. Japanese robe

S K X I Z M C O G N J O
2   9

6. salad in Japanese

H S O A R T A K D J A I
7   1

COMPLETE THE SENTENCE:

Japan is known as the Land of the

___ ___ ___ ___ ___ ___
 1   2   3   4   5   6

___ ___ ___
 7   8   9

Name _______________________________________ Date _______________________

GREAT WALL

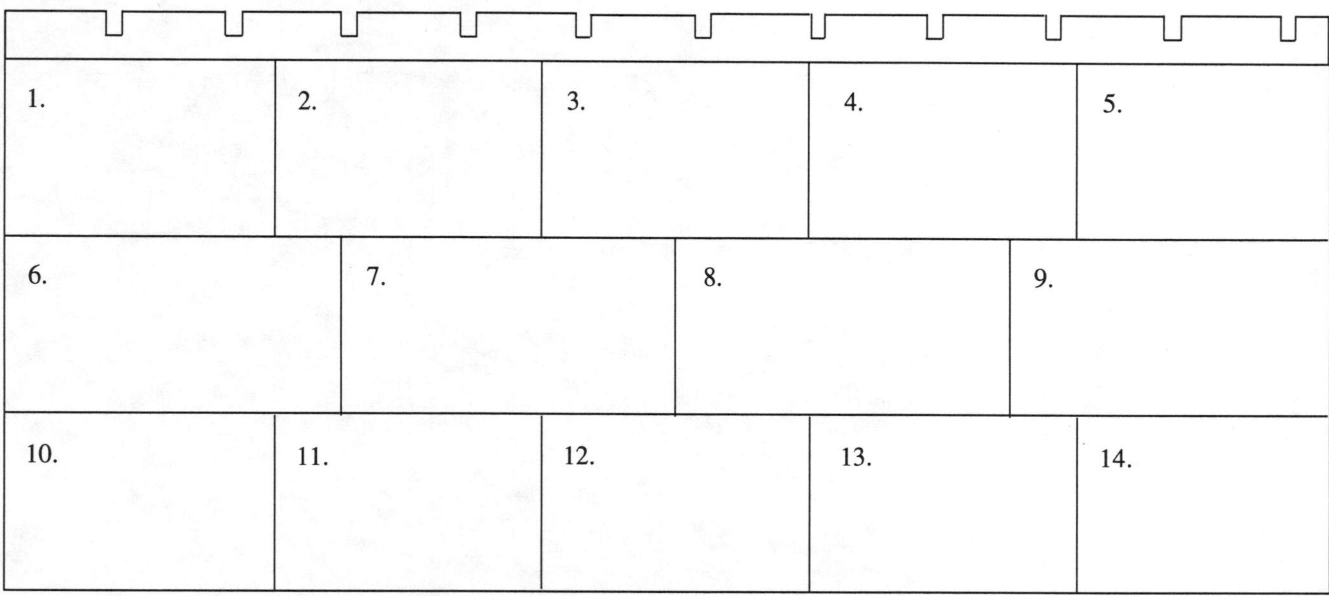

Complete the wall by filling in the blocks.
Each block should contain the response to the numbered clues:

1. number of characters
   in Chinese

2. draw the Chinese character
   for *mountain*

3. pinyin spelling for
   good-bye

4. number of people who speak
   Mandarin Chinese

5. period of time when emperors
   of the same family ruled

6. draw the Chinese character
   for *rain*

7. draw the Chinese character
   for *sun*

8. number of characters an
   average Chinese person knows

9. system that aids in
   pronunciation ("spell sound")

10. the great river that flows
    through China

11. pinyin spelling for
    good morning

12. draw the Chinese character
    for *person*

13. Chinese holiday in late
    January or early February

14. capital of China

Name ____ Date ___________

ANSWER IN ARABIC

Read the questions and situations in the box below. How would you respond to them in Arabic?
Put the letter of each situation next to the appropriate Arabic response to it.

A. Your friend from Algeria gave you some baklawa.

B. Arabic is read left to right like English. Yes or No?

C. You encounter a friend on a street in Cairo.

D. The number of letters in the Arabic alphabet is 28.

E. You open the door and invite your friend from Oman into your home.

F. The Arabic alphabet is the most widely used in the world. Yes or No?

G. You are wondering how a friend is feeling.

H. You are taking leave of your friend.

___________ 1. أهلا و سهلا (ahlan wa-sahlan)

___________ 2. كيف حالك؟ (keef halak)

___________ 3. السلام عليكم (as-salaam alaykom)

___________ 4. مع السلامة (maa al salaama)

___________ 5. نعم (naam)

___________ 6. لا (la)

___________ 7. شكرا (shookran)

Name ____ Date _________________

WHAT DO YOU KNOW ABOUT THE HEBREW LANGUAGE?

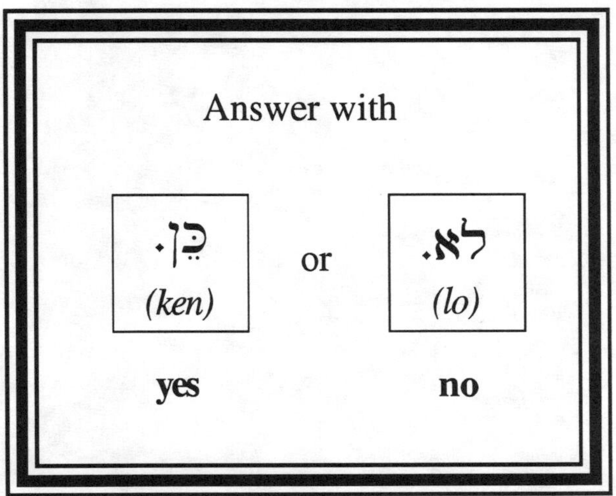

_________________ 1. "Shalom" means "peace," "hello," and "good-bye."

_________________ 2. The Hebrew alphabet has twenty-two consonants.

_________________ 3. Shabbat is a unit of money in Israel.

_________________ 4. The two official languages of Israel are Hebrew and English.

_________________ 5. Israel used to be called Palestine.

_________________ 6. The Hebrew language is two thousand years old.

_________________ 7. In a kibbutz, everyone shares things equally.

_________________ 8. The Hebrew calendar is based on the cycles of the moon.

_________________ 9. Israel became an independent country four thousand years ago.

_______________10. Rosh Hashanah and Yom Kippur are important Jewish holidays.

Name ____ Date _______________

SWAHILI SECRET MESSAGE

Look at the English clues in the box below, and fill in the crossword puzzles with the corresponding Swahili expressions. Complete the puzzle, and a secret message will be revealed.

Across
1. no
2. you're welcome
3. one
4. thank you
5. ten
6. two
7. yes
8. seven
9. harvest
10. together
11. freedom
12. good-bye
13. How are you?
14. nine

Name ____ Date _________________________

Latin in Our Language

Look at the *English word* in the left-hand column. Fill in the meaning of the *English word* in the middle column. Then, write the related Latin word in the right-hand column. Use a dictionary to help you find the answers.

	MEANING OF ENGLISH WORDS	LATIN
1. *amicable* relations	*friendly*	*amicus*
2. the town's *centennial* celebration		
3. *gratifying* to hear		
4. a *stellar* performance		
5. a *lunar* expedition		
6. the *quartet* of singers		
7. *uniquely* the first number		
8. the salesperson's *territory*		

Name ____ Date _______________________

GETTING TO THE ROOT OF GREEK

Draw a simple sketch or symbol that expresses the meaning of each Greek word part. In the spaces, write three English words that contain that part. Use a dictionary if you need help.

bio-	**metr-**	**hydro-**	**tele-**

graph-	**astron-**	**geo-**	**photo-**

NTC ELEMENTARY LANGUAGE TEXTS AND MATERIAL

Multilingual Resources
Basic Vocabulary Builder
Practical Vocabulary Builder
Language Visuals
NTC Language Posters
NTC Language Puppets
NTC Language Learning Flash Cards

Spanish
¡Viva el español!
  Learning Systems A, B, C
  Converso mucho
  Ya converso más
  ¡Nos comunicamos!
Welcome to Spanish
  First Start in Spanish
  Moving Ahead in Spanish
Spanish for Young Americans
  Hablan los niños
  Hablan más los niños
  Bienvenidos
Diccionario Bilingüe Ilustrado
Mi primera fonética
Mi cuaderno Workbooks 1, 2, 3
Aprendamos español Picture
  Dictionary
Let's Learn Spanish Picture Dictionary
Spanish Picture Dictionary
My First Spanish and English
  Dictionary
Let's Learn Spanish Coloring Book
Let's Learn Spanish Coloring Book-
  Audiocassette Package
My World in Spanish Coloring Book
Let's Learn about Spain
Ya sé leer and Ya sé leer Workbook
Leamos un cuento
Spanish and Bilingual Readers
  Horas encantadas
  Había una vez
  Mother Goose on the Rio Grande
  ¡Hola amigos! Series
  Treasury of Children's Classics in
    Spanish and English
  Bilingual Fables
  Historietas en español
  Gabriel, the Happy Ghost
Soundsalive Spanish Phonics Review
  Cards
Sounds and Letters Audio-Visual
  Ronda del alfabeto
  A, E, I, O, U: Ahora cantas tú

"Cantando" We Learn (songbook and
  cassette)
La Navidad
Christmas in Spain
Christmas in Mexico
El alfabeto

French
Aventures 1, 2
Comment ça va? Learning Package
Comment ça va? Song Cassette
Quand tu seras grand Song Cassette
Le loup du Nord Song Cassette
Let's Learn French Picture Dictionary
French Picture Dictionary
Let's Learn French Coloring Book
Let's Learn French Coloring
  Book-Audiocassette Package
My World in French Coloring Book
Let's Learn about France
Je lis, tu lis
Exercices en français facile
Il était une fois
Bilingual Fables
Noël
Christmas in France
L'alphabet

German
Let's Learn German Picture Dictionary
German Picture Dictionary
Let's Learn German Coloring Book
Let's Learn German Coloring Book-
  Audiocassette Package
My World in German Coloring Book
Let's Learn about Germany
Es War Einmal
Weihnacht
Christmas in Germany

Japanese
Japanese for Children
Konnichi wa, Japan

Italian
Let's Learn Italian Picture Dictionary
Let's Learn Italian Coloring Book
Let's Learn Italian Coloring Book-
  Audiocassette Package
My World in Italian Coloring Book
Let's Learn about Italy
The Story Teller
II Natale
Christmas in Italy

For further information or a current catalog, write:
National Textbook Company
a division of *NTC Publishing Group*
4255 West Touhy Avenue
Lincolnwood, Illinois 60646-1975 U.S.A.